THE UNIVERSITY OF GRAVEL ROADS

GLOBAL LESSONS FROM A FOUR-YEAR MOTORCYCLE ADVENTURE

RENE CORMIER

MARVIN,
all the best for your
future gravel road adventures!

Rene

Published by Renedian Adventures Ltd. 2010
www.renedian.com

Copyright © 2010 Rene Cormier

First printed in Canada, 2010.
Second printing, Canada, 2011.

Library and Archives Canada Cataloguing in Publication
Cormier, Rene, 1970-
      The university of gravel roads : global lessons from a four-year motorcycle adventure / Rene Cormier.
ISBN 978-0-9813371-1-1
1. Cormier, Rene, 1970- --Travel. 2. Motorcycle touring. 3. Voyages around the world. I. Title.
G465.C65 2010   910.4'1092   C2009-906571-1

Cover and interior design: Swanie
Editor and proofreader: Jennifer Groundwater. Edited using contemporary Canadian spelling.

Photo Credits:
Amy Bruning: 29 (lower left), 29 (upper right), 35 (all)
Brigitte Cormier: 44
Daren McDonald: 62
Marleen Bauween: 79, 80 (bottom), 81, 84, back cover
Robert Allan: 92 (bottom), 100 (bottom), 101 (left), 105 (bottom right), 106 (upper right)
Michael Narozny: 100 (top)
Johan Claassens: 108 (both)
Paul Brooks: 140, 144 (bottom right)
Drew Sagar: 157 (upper left)

Maps pages 4, 8, 12, 24, 64, 98, 118, 134, 152 reproduced courtesy of The World Factbook 2009. Washington, DC: Central Intelligence Agency, 2009.
Map page 6 reproduced courtesy of the University of Texas Libraries, The University of Texas at Austin.
Map page 38 reproduced courtesy of the Department of National Resources, Canada.

CONTENTS

PROLOGUE 1

1992

I n 1992, I was a university biology student taking external studies courses while on safari in Kenya's wonderful parks. We were 56 students crammed into a nose to tail convoy of seven minivans. Through the dust near Lake Baringo, my eyes focused on a group of three BMW motorcycles grossly overloaded with spare tires and jerry cans of fuel going the other way. From my much too small seat in the van I perked up at my first glimpse of a motorcycle being used for adventure travel. *This* was the way to do it! This was independent travel at its liberated best.

I stared out of the window and daydreamt about how much better travelling by motorcycle would be: no queuing for bus tickets, struggling with train timetables, or being at the mercy of a public transportation system that did not care much about the public it was transporting. The motorcycle would be at home on dirt roads, highways, and trails. It was faster than a bicycle, but not as hermetically sealed as a car. The limited carrying capacity forced the luggage down to its most basic elements, and any subsequent needs would be sorted out on the road with a healthy dollop of creativity.

Being a penniless student, I did not fool myself that the motoring lifestyle that had just passed us would be available to me anytime soon, but perhaps someday....

2003

I slept on the sand under a million desert stars, a half-finished beer leaning against my motorcycle's tire. My dreams were interrupted by a loud *crack* and the smell of gasoline. I turned on my small camping headlight and saw gas pouring from the engine area onto my sleeping bag. I scrambled up and tried to trace the source of the leak. Out of the corner of my eye, I saw a set of headlights a few hundred metres to the west, back on the gravel road. The vehicle was not moving and I gradually came to the annoying realization that its occupants were shooting at me. The loud noise that woke me was the sound of bullet ripping through the plastic gas tank, leaving a pea-sized hole.

Two weeks earlier my friends had warned me about all the trouble I might encounter as I tried to drive my BMW motorcycle around the world: *banditos* in Mexico, drug lords in Colombia, and the mafia in Russia. But there I was, in Utah's desert, trying to make it to Canada to *start* the trip, and I was getting shot at. What a way to start an adventure.

CHAPTER 1
The Idea

Ten years after I first saw those motorbikes at Lake Baringo I had the world by the tail. I had bubbled my way up in the bicycle industry and found myself as the Communication Manager of Colorado-based RockShox, a large suspension manufacturer for bicycles. In this lucky position I rode bicycles and drank beer with journalists from all over the world – and called it work.

In August of 2002, I planned my first multi-week trip on a motorcycle, a one-month affair from Colorado Springs to the Arctic Circle in Alaska. I would be riding the first motorcycle I ever owned, a used 1986 BMW R100 GSPD, the same model that I had seen in Kenya. Shortly before I left, RockShox announced that it was to be purchased by a Chicago-based firm and that many positions, including mine, were to be relocated there. I declined the position and gave the company notice that I would stay until the end of 2002 to help with the transition and then return to Canada. Making this decision was a welcome weight off of my shoulders and I looked forward to a month on the motorcycle to daydream about what might come next for me.

The time away would also allow me to think about Amy, a girl I had met the week before I was due to depart. The timing for the start of a relationship was far from perfect – our first dates were spent talking about the unromantic subjects of the solo trip to Alaska or my returning to Canada. One of the first phone messages I received while on the road was from Amy, letting me know that she had read about a technique to tell one's horoscope by massaging their butt, and she wanted to try it. I couldn't let a girl like that get away.

In Alaska, the long days of summer riding and the good roads allowed hours of contemplation of my new soon-to-be-unemployed state. As a Canadian working in the United States on a temporary visa, I would not be able to stay and look for another job, so I would be returning to Canada at some point soon to do something new. But what would it be?

In a ferry lineup in Alaska, I met Mauricio and Eduardo, two quiet BMW riders from Colombia, who provided me with the answer. We enjoyed a three-day, three-boxes-of-red-wine ferry ride together from Alaska to Washington State, during which they convinced me that what I needed to do was to take the motorcycle to South America for a year. Their arguments were compelling: the weather was great, Spanish was easy to learn and spoken almost everywhere, the women were beautiful, and if you were willing to camp and rough it a bit, it was cheap as well.

On the ride home from Washington it occurred to me that this was the only time in my life where the conditions would be right for taking a longer trip, perhaps even a trip around the world. I had always known that there would never be a morning when I would wake up with nothing to do for the year and a whack of cash in the bank. But now I had a big blank spot coming up in my calendar. That just left the question of finding finances to support the venture. I admittedly had no idea how much such a ride would cost, but I was sure that with a bit of time on the internet, I could find out.

Amy was waiting for me as I pulled into the driveway. I waited a day before telling her that I was taking a year off to do a solo circumnavigation of the earth.

Looking at the atlas it became apparent that although it may be possible to drive around the world in a year (in fact, the Guinness world record for this feat was a little over 19 days), that was not the type of ride that I wanted. I was not rich enough to travel for a decade, so somewhere between 19 days and ten years would be the length of time for my trip. The simple way to figure out the exact length was to add up how much money I had available for the trip, and divide it by the cost of living per day while travelling.

I wrote down all the items I had that could be sold to generate cash. My house, books, skis, other motorcycles, and clothes were all up for sale; I estimated that selling all of these could raise $50,000[1]. My internet research told me that a $25 daily allowance for gas, food, and camping was as low as would be comfortable without resorting to eating other people's leftovers or always sleeping under bridges. Spending $25 a day for a year added up to $9125, and allowing for irregular costs such as airline tickets, annual health insurance, and transport of the motorcycle from one continent to another, my fifty grand would theoretically allow me to travel for three solid years with a little left over in an emergency fund.

I decided on an ambitious three-year trip doing North and South America in a year, then Africa to Russia, then on to Australia and New Zealand for the last two years. I then told as many people as I could about my plan to help prevent me from getting cold feet and backing out.

January 1, 2003 was my last official day at work. I now had four months to sell all of my belongings and prepare the motorcycle and the gear for the trip. Despite our looming separation, the relationship between Amy

and me had grown stronger. One evening she sent me an email expressing her desire to join me on the trip. She was recently widowed, having lost her husband in an auto accident the year before I met her. She was painfully aware of how quickly life changed and although she did not say as much in the email, I sensed that she felt it was time to take a chance with life again and open her sails to the wind. From then on, our planning focused on the logistics of a shared trip.

Amy would be riding her own bike, and the only one that fit her was the lowered version of the popular BMW F650GS. The golden rule of travelling with multiple bikes is to keep them as similar as possible. This allows you to consolidate tools and spare parts, and makes troubleshooting easier should one of the bikes develop a problem. If Amy fit the F650GS, then the bike that would take me around the world would also be the F650GS, although I opted for the slightly taller Dakar version.

I hurried to sell my other two BMW bikes to generate cash for the trip. I was disappointed to sell my 1150GS for $12,500 when I had bought it for $18,000 just five months earlier. I lost money on the R100, too. The amount I hoped to have for my trip was shrinking before my over-optimistic eyes. As the selling continued, I was shocked when my new ski gear also fetched a fraction of the amount I had paid only months before. I had not even started my trip, and the life lessons had already begun to pile on. What a waste to be paying so much on depreciation! Why buy anything new ever again?

I answered my own question when a search of Colorado and the surrounding states found no used F650GS Dakars on the market. I sheepishly resorted to buying a new one.

Three months remained for me to equip the bike with travelling gear and learn about the basic maintenance that I would need to perform. Many of the countries that I planned to visit did not have any BMW presence and that meant that I needed to become my own mechanic, which was not a skill that came naturally.

Amy started her exit-from-normal-life plan by putting her house on the market and buying her motorcycle. She had driven a motorcycle for a

[1] All prices in USD.

grand total of ten minutes in her entire life. I spent early mornings teaching her how to start and stop the bike and how the gears work by driving up and down the alley behind her house. Soon, she was taking very early morning rides around town. Her confidence grew with every outing.

The plan was for me to leave for Canada in April. At the same time, Amy would leave for her parents' home on the east coast of the USA to finish a lingering, almost-done master's degree. It would take Amy a year to wrap up her schooling and by then I would have completed my travels in South America. Amy and her motorcycle would meet me in Africa to continue the rest of the trip together.

My April trip from Colorado Springs to Vancouver was to be a shakedown trip to test packing methods. Along the way I stopped in Utah to meet up with Amy and her friend who had just finished a five-day hike. Soon after our visit there a solo hiker had his hand trapped by a shifting boulder, and the only way to free himself was to amputate his own arm with a jackknife. To me, this story was a not-so-subtle reminder of the risks associated with solo travel...and a reminder to purchase travel insurance.

The concept of travel insurance came up again a few days later when I was shot at in the desert. The next morning, I found Sheriff Stephen Allred in the quiet town of Delta, Utah, and explained what had happened the previous night. He took notes about the incident, but let me know that the chances of finding these people would be "somewhere between slim and none." He went on to say

Sheriff Allred helps gather evidence.

that there were people who go out at night into the desert to shoot coyotes and rabbits.

"And tourists," I reminded him. We fished the slug out of the tank and although the bullet was deformed from the impact, we could tell it was a .22 caliber.

I was now more bummed about the daunting cost of replacing the tank, which I estimated at around $700 a side.

After filling out the sheriff's paperwork, I headed north to Vancouver to complete my final preparations.

Bullet hole.

Immunizations were $800 worth of tetanus/diphtheria, Japanese encephalitis, hepatitis A, hepatitis B, yellow fever, rabies, meningitis, plus boosters for polio and measles and mumps.

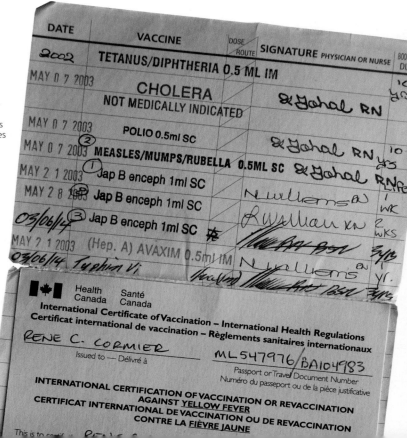

CANADA
UNITED STATES
ROCKY MOUNTAINS
APPALACHIAN MOUNTAINS
NORTH PACIFIC OCEAN
NORTH ATLANTIC OCEAN
MID-ATLANTIC RIDGE
Hudson Bay
Labrador Sea
Island of Newfoundland
Gulf of Mexico
Caribbean Sea
Tropic of Cancer (23°27')
MEXICO
Ottawa
Montreal
Boston
New York
Philadelphia
Washington, D.C.
Atlanta
Miami
Chicago
Detroit
Minneapolis
Denver
Dallas
San Francisco
Los Angeles
Tijuana
Edmonton
Seattle
Havana
CUBA
THE BAHAMAS
Nassau
Bermuda
JAMAICA
Kingston
HAITI
DOMINICAN REPUBLIC
Santo Domingo
Puerto Rico
BELIZE
Belmopan
HONDURAS
GUATEMALA
EL SALVADOR
San Salvador
NICARAGUA
Managua
COSTA RICA
San José
PANAMA
VENEZUELA
Caracas
COLOMBIA
Bogotá
ECUADOR
Quito
GUYANA
Georgetown
SURINAME
Paramaribo
French Guiana
Cayenne
Clipperton Island
GALAPAGOS ISLANDS
Nuuk (Godthåb)
CAPE VERDE
Praia

CHAPTER 2

NORTH AND CENTRAL AMERICA

I arrived in Vancouver with a long to-do list. Days were spent on the computer looking for health insurance policies, selling the last of my goods in Colorado via the internet, and sealing the hole in the gas tank. I also learned about the formidable world of carnets. A carnet is a type of security deposit for a motorcycle that allows its driver to import it temporarily into a country without paying import duties or taxes. Some countries are unconcerned about the entry of foreign vehicles, while others are very worried that the vehicles will be illegally sold, thereby depriving the government of the import taxes that normally come with a vehicle sale. Since different countries have different import taxes, the value of the carnet is based on the rate for the most expensive country on your list of countries to visit, as this amount automatically covers all of the less expensive countries as well.

On my list, Iran requested the highest deposit, at 120% of the value of the bike. I would have to deposit this amount in cash with the Canadian Automobile Association (CAA) as a promise that the motorcycle would come back to Canada. I argued with the CAA that the value of the motorcycle should not be "as-new," since it already had several thousand kilometres and a bullet hole in it. They replied that I should get an appraisal of the motorcycle from a BMW dealership and they would review the cost. I made a mental note to get the appraisal done just before I left eastern Canada for the USA, when the bike would have slightly higher mileage.

I created a very basic website and I started to figure out the Sony Mavica camera I had bought before I left Colorado. It was a four megapixel camera that cost me $500, and I liked it because it took video, and also because it did not use memory cards. The images were recorded onto a 156 MB mini CD that I could remove and insert into the computer at any internet café. I changed the quality settings to "low" in order to cram the most number of pictures onto a disk, a thrifty decision I would come to regret.

By June, my education in route planning and trip logistics was far from complete, and I realized that there was no way that I would be able to prepare adequately for the entire trip in advance. My plan was still to get to the bottom of South America for the New Year's celebration in six months. I had hoped that Mauricio in Colombia would be able to assist with the planning for many of the routes in South America, but my emails to him went unanswered.

Although I had left Colorado two months earlier, June 10, 2003 was the first official travel day of the trip. Day 1 of 1000. During my planning, I had always envisioned my exact starting location as the parking lot for Kitsilano Beach and its outdoor pool. The pool was one of my all-time favorite places and it seemed fitting to leave from there. Since I was

The bike ready to go.

alone, I approached a stranger in the parking lot and asked if he could take a photo of me.

With that formality out of the way, I was off, overloaded and overwhelmed.

Once on the road, I thought often of the wisdom of this trip from the point of view of financial security. Newspapers told about the benefits of investing into the property market. If I invested wisely, I could retire early. My friends discussed stock options, bigger houses, newer cars, better wine, or fancier schools for their kids. I was about to take my little nest egg and suck it dry on a trip which I had no idea how to do properly. This was not a fiscally prudent move. It flew in the face of what was deemed a safe and responsible investment strategy from those who equate personal comfort with personal equity.

For the next 1000 days I needed to buy gas, buy food, and find places to sleep in countries that I had never been to before. My budget did not allow me the option of pulling into an international hotel every night to a familiar haven of English-speaking receptionists, CNN on the television, and clean white sheets. I saw myself repeatedly standing in the wrong line to pay too much for the wrong thing. And when I returned – what then? If all went according to plan, I would return at 36 years old with little money and no recent working history. Not the most attractive of circumstances to go job-hunting with or to start off a new career.

I arrived in New Brunswick a week after leaving Vancouver. In one of the most courageous rides of the trip, Amy battled interstate traffic and rain to make a three-day solo trip from Pennsylvania to Canada to meet me. She couldn't claim to be a novice rider any more. It was Amy's first time in Canada as well as her first time on a long motorcycle trip, and it was my first time travelling with another motorcycle. We toured Canada's

Maritime provinces for a month, returning to New Brunswick for a family reunion. Over drinks one night we got into the conversation about

Cape Bonavista lighthouse, Newfoundland.

THE UNIVERSITY OF GRAVEL ROADS

Amy drove from Pennsylvania to meet me in New Brunswick, a heroic three-day solo trip in itself for a new rider.

naming our motorcycles. We called Amy's bike "Timbit" after a small donut available in Canada and Amy suggested "Q-tip" for my bike, playing off my obsession with cleaning my ears, but I vetoed it and the bike remained nameless.

As August wound down, I needed to get on the road south if I was going to make the bottom of Argentina in four months. The last item on my to-do list was to get the appraisal of the motorcycle done so I could complete the carnet paperwork.

Our cottage was twenty minutes from the city and the highway split large tracts of forest to get there. As I drove towards town to get the appraisal, I startled three deer that were grazing in the right-hand ditch. Two of the deer bolted deeper into the forest, while the third ran alongside the road in the same direction that I was going. This third deer suddenly took a hard left and tried to cross the road in front of me. I slammed both brakes hard and concentrated on bringing the speed of the bike down and continuing in a straight line. My only hope was that the deer's trajectory was not going to intersect with mine. Seeing a big wall of brown suggested that it was.

I closed my eyes, relaxed my grip on the bars, and waited for the impact. I felt the front of the bike drop out from under me as I flew over the top of the windscreen. I landed on my right shoulder and had enough presence of mind to roll out of it as I had learned in judo lessons when I was eight years old. My initial shock wore off quickly as a van stopped behind me and helped me get the bike onto the side of the road.

I was wearing my full motorcycle jacket with padding, pants with padding, leather gloves, and a helmet, and this gear had mitigated the damage to me greatly. At first glance I only had a sore right shoulder and miscellaneous road rash. My jacket had worn through on the upper back, and my helmet was cracked. A tow truck came and I gave instructions to take the bike to the BMW dealer while the ambulance took me to the hospital for x-rays and a checkup. I used the nurses' phone to call the cottage. My sister answered the phone and I spoke quietly to her.

"First of all, you need to know I am fine. Secondly, I just hit a deer and am in the hospital only because they want to take a precautionary look. Can you ask Dad to come and get me? And don't tell Amy."

I did not need Amy worked up and upset, and I figured I could let her know about the accident in person when Dad and I arrived back at the cottage.

This would have been a successful plan, except Amy did come to the hospital with Dad and saw me laid out on a stretcher with a big white neck brace on and my shirt and motorcycle jacket shredded.

"I'm going to kill you if you ever get better," she threatened, her eyes red and voice unsteady. Smiling, she continued softly, "You boys can't keep doing this to me." She held my hand tightly until the

Damage from the deer collision.

x-rays came back confirming that the damage was limited to the right shoulder, left hand, and a bit of bruising on my legs.

With a sling holding my arm firmly in place, we returned to the cottage and I scrapped the idea of getting to Argentina in four months. In an instant, the trip's schedule had been thrown out the window, and I added six months to the original plan. Amy and I celebrated our one-year anniversary over maps and discussions about South America, as it seemed that our best option now was to meet in South America when her schooling was done.

The front end of the bike had been damaged in the crash, and it took two weeks for replacement parts to arrive. A close look at my jacket told the story of it working well to protect my skin from my slide on the asphalt. A new Aerostich jacket was over $500, money that I wanted to spend on travelling, not clothes, so I took the jacket to a boot repair shop and we picked out heavy, black waterproof fabric that they sewed onto the shredded areas. The repair was functional and did not look bad, and like the gas tank fix in Vancouver, I was pleased with making the fix-it choice between repairing and replacing.

Amy returned to Pennsylvania alone. I had been scheduled to make the journey with her, but was still unable to ride. She made it home without concern in three days to find the cat skinny, the dog fat, and a school term waiting.

One upside of the accident with the deer was that the value of the motorcycle for the carnet was definitely lower. With mileage of 15,000 kilometres, a bullet hole, and a head-on collision with a deer as evidence, the BMW dealership appraised the bike at $6400, making my carnet deposit $7680.

Once this paperwork was sorted out, I left Canada, not expecting to return for three years. But I did not get very far. Suspicious American border guards detained me as I attempted to enter Maine. Driving into the USA with a motorcycle loaded with personal goods raised a red flag, even though I explained that I was just passing through on my way to Mexico. After Mexicans, Canadians are the largest group of illegal workers in America and they wanted to verify my story. I showed them bank statements, investment statements, and my website that described the preparation and trip layout. After an hour of show and tell, they reluctantly let me go.

I realized why many Americans preferred to travel only within America: with a wide selection of roads, gunfire, interrogative border crossings, kind strangers, lunatics, and foreign languages, all the aspects of global adventure travel can already be found there.

The cost of travel in the USA was higher than my daily $25 budget could support for an extended time, and winter was on my heels, so my plan was to make a quick visit to Amy in Pennsylvania and enter Mexico in January.

My stay with Amy was two days of planning, maps and getting her bike sorted out. Her ride back from Canada had been smooth and she was noticeably more comfortable on the bike with each mile that she successfully negotiated. We spent quiet time together, knowing that the next time we would see each other would be in Ecuador nine months later, and we both recognized the potential of this time apart to chill our relationship. We had only known each other for a year and I had been away for a large part of that time on the bike. Surviving the nine-month gap and then travelling with each other for three years around the world would be a considerable test of our compatibility.

My below-freezing Christmas campsite at a trailer park in Lafayette, Louisiana was made bearable by the discovery of notes written by Amy hidden in my luggage and by an email from AJ, a friend from the bicycle industry. He would be in the small Mexican town of San Felipe over New Year's Eve and he invited me to join him if I could make it over in time.

On the last day of 2003, I filled up with a hearty breakfast at Bubba's Southern BBQ in Yuma, Arizona, got Mexican motorcycle insurance, and dashed off to the border. I was concerned that the border formalities would be difficult to negotiate, but the officials were friendly and helpful and within an hour I was through.

The Mexican landscape was immediately different; poorer, to be sure, but not at all disorganized. Although it was dirty and there was refuse everywhere, it all worked in an industrial fashion. I made it down to San Felipe in the early afternoon and went to the hotel where AJ was staying.

The hotelkeeper told me AJ was in town but let me into the room so I could unpack the bike and take a shower. In typical desert fashion, when the sun went down, the temperature plummeted. I turned on the small space heater and hunched over it until I heard a motorcycle return.

I went outside to greet AJ, and instead found two of his friends, whose room I had been relaxing in. They had all been riding together the previous day, but AJ had had a last-minute change of plans and had headed back to the USA a few hours earlier.

I apologized for crashing in their room and sheepishly asked if they minded if I slept on their floor for the night. With our energy spent from long days riding, we elected not to go to the bar and celebrate and by 11 p.m. our lights were out.

By 8 a.m. I was packed and headed south. It was my first day on the road in a foreign-speaking country and I had many more to go. I did not have enough Spanish to ask how things worked, so at my first fuel stop I got off the bike and waited for the attendant to come over and fill the bike. He did, so I gathered that this was a full-service place. I watched his actions carefully, having heard many stories about how they will not zero the pump before they start filling the bike or some other crafty way of shafting the tourist. It all looked normal, and I looked at the digital readout on the pump to find out the price in pesos. I tried doing the currency conversion in my head to make sure I was not paying hundreds of dollars for five dollars' worth of gas but soon gave up, offering a handful of notes to the attendant to pick out what he needed.

During the first few weeks on Mexican roads, I noticed a pattern emerging in my thoughts. Before noon, everything was carefree and light. As the afternoon started, I would begin to worry about where I was going to sleep that night. Once the basics of shelter and security were sorted, my thoughts turned to food. Once I had eaten, thoughts turned to the road ahead and where I was going to get gas. Rarely did my mind stop stressing about something. A worry that had been solved moved aside to allow a new one to settle in.

After a month of travel, however, the mental pattern slowly but noticeably began to change. My Spanish words were coming along, and I knew that every 100 kilometres I could find gas. I knew how the gasoline filling procedure went, and my currency conversion was honed enough to give me the knowledge of how much I should be paying. I was never ripped off by any of the gas station attendants, or anyone else for that matter. I had found a place to sleep every night, some nicer than others, but all were acceptable. I also never had a problem finding food. My eating problems were limited to ordering too much delicious food from street vendors and trying to find a way to store it on the motorcycle for a later snack. Logic and experience slowly made me realize that these patterns would continue and that I could find food and shelter without much effort.

Lunch was always just a market away.

An overnight ferry took me from Baja California to the Mexican mainland city of Mazatlán on my 34th birthday. It seemed to me that Mazatlán had grown immensely since I was there when I was 18. That trip had been my first solo vacation outside of Canada; I flew down without hotel reservations or a word of Spanish, and everything worked out fine. I often thought about that first travel experience when I arrived somewhere new on the motorcycle. I did not know how a situation was going to turn out, but I knew it would turn out somehow. I just needed to keep nudging the process in the direction of the outcome that I wanted most.

To keep alert and practise my Spanish, I read the road signs and talked to myself daily. I asked the questions that I regularly used when ordering food, fuel, or beer. When I was familiar with the questions, I practised the multiple choices for the answer, so I would not be overwhelmed by words I had never heard before. With time my Spanish became better and I tried to speak quickly so I would sound as if I had been speaking Spanish all my life. It was a tactic that I schemed up, thinking that if somebody overheard me speaking complete sentences in rapid-fire Spanish, then I wouldn't seem like a new tourist. This way, I would be less of a target for all of the banditos that many Canadians and Americans had warned me about, but I had yet to find.

I avoided the expensive toll roads and wound my way slowly south on a variety of paved secondary roads as finding dirt roads were more difficult than I had anticipated. What was easier was the navigation in town. Every Mexican town has a church in the middle of it; across the street from the church is the square plaza with trees, grass, and benches. In the cool air of evening, kids and families gather to enjoy music and food from the vendors who set up stalls here. On the streets around the plaza are the banks and expensive hotels, but as you walk away from the plaza, the prices of the hotels drop, and you can keep walking until you hit your budget. Fortunately for me, the main highway often brought me very near to the plazas in the smaller towns, which eliminated the need for detailed maps.

My nights at the plazas were among my most enjoyable in Mexico. Traditional music moved me so much that I bought a guitar. I did not know how to play it, but I loved the sound and I figured I had two and a half more years of travelling to learn. Relaxed evenings made it difficult not to fall in love with the pace of rural Mexican life. A respect for elders was very present, and it was unheard-of to pass an older man or lady without wishing them a good afternoon or good evening. Their returned greetings came with a smile and were pronounced slowly and carefully for the benefit of my foreign ears.

During one nightly wander around the plaza I ran into a group of *callejoneadas*, who were musicians that revived an old tradition from Spain that involved singing, dancing, wandering the street, and getting progres-

Small town plazas come alive in the cool of the evening.

sively drunker. My guidebook was very complete in these matters.

When I arrived, the group of about 70 or so had just started moving. Most had little pottery jars around their necks tied with a nice ribbon. I couldn't see where they had gotten these, so I grabbed a Styrofoam cup from a local café and hopped into the crowd. The crowd was led by a ten-man band, mostly trumpets, drums and trombones. Behind the band was the burro. The burro was important because it carried the mescal that was continuously poured into the little cups around one's neck, unless one had a Styrofoam cup, in which case that was filled. (The Styrofoam cup held considerably more than the little pottery jars.)

The band played and wandered wherever they wanted: up and down alleys, across main streets, stopping traffic, backwards, or forwards. All the time they were playing, and more often than not they were throwing their hats around. The musicians, especially the trumpeters, liked to blast their music into the open windows of houses, cars, and restaurants.

Our last stop was in the plaza in front of the Museum of Abstract Art. We arrived as a rather wobbly bunch. Instantly there was a queue at the taco stand that was set up there. I thought it quite clever that the band and the taco guy worked together, as I was starving by this point. The ravenous horde went right to the cart. I got in line, loaded up with a heaping plate of fish tacos and beans, and sat down with a group that I had said hi to earlier.

"Do you know what this celebration is?" they asked.

"Yes," and I proudly started to quote my guidebook to inform them of the colourful history of the callejoneadas.

"No. This is a wedding."

That explained the finely dressed people and why the taco guy did not take my money when I tried to pay for my food.

"Oops – so sorry!" I was more than a little embarrassed that I had crashed the wedding, but they would have none of my apologies. Within minutes I had met the bride and groom and their families, and was invited to the bigger party that was happening the following night. I graciously declined, hoping that I was not committing a serious cultural faux pas, but the vernal equinox was coming and I wanted to be celebrating it on the pyramids of Teotihuacán near Mexico City.

The archeological site of Teotihuacán held the impressive Pyramid of the Sun, the third largest pyramid in the world. It was built from three million tons of stone, brick, and rubble without the use of metal tools, pack animals, or the wheel, and was quite possibly surrounded by one of the largest cities in the world at that time. I thought it was entirely appropriate to get up early and catch the equinox sunrise from the top of a structure built to honour the sun gods 2000 years earlier.

The last time I tried getting up this ridiculously early to see the sunrise was with Amy in Cape Spear, Newfoundland, the most easterly point in North America. Here the sun rises before anywhere else in North and Central America, but when we drove to the rocky cape, all we saw were sheets of grey fog getting lighter and lighter and not much sun. I hoped not to be skunked again here.

Predawn at the Pyramid of the Sun, Teotihuacán.

The morning of the equinox was clear with a temperature not much higher than freezing, and I splurged on a $2 cab ride from the plaza to the park at 4:45 a.m. I had expected the place to be deserted, but found the parking lots packed with mostly younger folks. Hundreds of small fires burned around their tents, and bongo drummers and street vendors worked under the temporary lights set up along the main entryway. Vendors sold coffee with cinnamon, mole tamales made with a deliciously spicy chocolate sauce, and salty fried crickets.

I wandered down the dark streets of the ancient city toward the base of the mammoth pyramid to the east of the complex. Dawn started to break night's hold on the sky and deep blues crept in from the eastern horizon. The wind was biting on the ground, but I figured I could shiver at the top just as well and proceeded to head up the pyramid. Trickles of light ascended the 248 stairs to the summit as people's flashlights zigged and zagged with their steps.

When I got to the top, there was barely enough room to stand. I wasn't the only one who wanted to see the sunrise from the summit, but most of these folks had spent the night at the top, hiding from the wind, bundled in blankets and sleeping bags, and peeing in empty Coke bottles like the truck drivers do. The top level was about 1000 square feet and was surfaced with slightly domed fist-sized rocks set in concrete, which made finding a level and comfortable spot to sit a challenge. I made my way slowly to the centre of the crowd, enjoying the windbreak created by the other people.

At 6:15 a.m. there was a procession that included two women carrying incense burners; one contained sage, the other had something sweet-smelling but unidentifiable to me. They came from the stairs on the west side, and proceeded to the east. They walked with a few priests and a small group to the middle of the east-facing ledge, and set upon the ground various swatches of fabric and corn upon the fabric. The priest talked and we held our hands up towards where the sun was creeping up, not visible yet, but on its way. Then we held our hands up towards the west, north, and south in turn. Corn and pieces of fabric were placed in the handheld goblets that contained the burning incense. At the start of the priest's chanting a strong wind picked up and fanned the glowing embers in the goblet, spraying the crowd with a white stream of

ABOVE: Sunrise on top of the Pyramid of the Sun.

BELOW: Ancient blessings.

incense smoke and glowing ashes. I asked myself if the timing was only a coincidence.

According to the watch on the fellow next to me, the sun came up at 6:40. The beams of light spilled over a small mountain in the east and slowly lowered towards us, as the clouds blossomed from blood-red to pink.

A lingering cloud denied us the first few precious moments of direct sun to warm our shivering group. I wondered what this delay in the sun's appearance would have meant 2000 years ago and how they might have interpreted it as a sign for the year ahead. What would the priests need to do to appease the gods and make amends to secure a year with bountiful crops and successful warfare?

Conch shells blew, a few whistles shrilled, and then silence settled on the top as people placed their arms in the sky, palms outward to catch the first of the vernal equinox rays. I sat facing the sun, eyes closed, listening to the wind whip nylon jackets around me, feeling the warmth on my face.

Before leading the procession down the pyramid, the priests handed out handfuls of blessed corn kernels, which were to be planted in the garden to ensure a bountiful crop. Looking down from the top, there was already a lineup at least a kilometre long waiting to get to where I was. By the time I left the complex in the early afternoon, this line had doubled in length.

The next day I received an email from the

CHAPTER 3
SOUTH AMERICA

Flying into Quito, I marvelled at the 35-kilometre length of the city, and when I climbed the airport stairs I appreciated the 2918-metre (9574 ft) elevation. I found a backpackers' hostel and waited the few days for Amy to arrive. To pass the time, I updated my budget spreadsheet, a task I thoroughly enjoyed doing. It provided me a chance to keep close tabs on my finances and extrapolate how much time I could still travel. The results were not always encouraging. I was doing very well in keeping to my $25-a-day goal, but the net amount of cash I had left only allowed for another two years of travel. The money was moving much quicker than I was.

Amy arrived on time and a little weary on June 1, and we spent our first days catching up on the last nine months. Drinking coffee, practicing Spanish, and walking through the old parts of Quito kept us occupied as we waited for Amy's bike to go through customs at the air cargo office.

Through a motorcycle website, we met Dan Walsh, a travelling journalist from the UK. The local pub culture was an important part of his writing research, so he was willing to meet there for a pint or two. He rode the same motorcycle as I did, although his looked like the bride of Frankenstein with its generous helpings of duct tape and road rash.

"I didn't do all that. I picked it up like that from the BMW Demo Fleet," he answered, without a hint of apology. He could not understand why, after only seeing each other five days in the last nine months, Amy and I would opt to sleep in the $5-a-night dorm beds instead of getting a private room for $14 a night. I explained that we had had the private room for three days of extravagance and now we were back to the dirtbag tour budget. Dan took pity on Amy and me and kindly bought us drinks all night, including a record number of "...just one more..." beers.

Quito offered glorious riding weather and as soon as the bikes were ready, we left the city. Amy quickly became familiar with oncoming cars overtaking each other in her lane, and other irregularities of driving in the developing world. Even though we were 20 kilometres from the equator, our altitude kept the temperature a pleasant 15-20C during the day, perfect for riding, and 10C at night, perfect for sleeping outside.

We crossed the equator to the famous Saturday market town of Otavalo and found our inaugural camping spot at a nearby lake. We had access to a small herb garden and we cobbled together a delicious soup with fresh, unknown vegetables picked up at the market. Amy had a great natural curiosity about food and enjoyed getting lost in the food markets. She discovered new and odd foods that looked cool but that we had no idea how to cook, including the local favourite, roasted guinea pig. While learning about new food was fascinating, it was also frustrating not to have a full kitchen to properly cook many of our discoveries. Our food preparation kit consisted of a small camping stove that ran on gasoline and two pots. To round out the kitchen we also had two coffee mugs, one set of cutlery each, and a cutting board that doubled as a plate. For ease of cooking and practicality, many meals started with a chicken stock cube and garlic, and from there turned into stews (if we had lots of veggies) or soups (if we had only a few, or none). Eggs were also available everywhere, but unlike back home, they were sold from the dry goods shelf, not the cooler. Avocadoes, tomatoes, and onions also made regular appearances at the markets, and we found freshly prepared guacamole to be an unexpected and inexpensive luxury while bush camping.

As much as we enjoyed cooking, there was no point in trying to make lunches for ourselves if we were anywhere near a town that had a covered

When I consulted a doctor friend about the medical precautions for my trip, we went through the details of familiar diseases such as malaria, dengue fever, tuberculosis, and schistosomiasis. He warned me that statistically, I was more likely to be involved in a motor vehicle accident than to catch malaria. Aggressive drivers, poorly maintained roads, wandering animals, nonroadworthy cars, and random debris like this crashed bus all lent support to his advice.

market. Inside were rows of waist-high, one-person kitchen stalls that served a set meal for lunch. These compact stalls allowed the cook to serve the two or three guests sitting on bar stools without stepping away from the stove. Soup and a rice dish were an inevitable part of the set menu, which was usually priced well under a dollar.

In the morning we started what would become an enjoyable daily exercise; mapping out the roads and the highlights for the day. Choosing our daily destinations followed relaxed guidelines; generally south and generally away from rain. Detours were always considered for hotsprings, mountain passes, and quiet back roads. We got lucky with planning our first full day on the road with the discovery of a town with hot springs not far away. We spent the day in first gear heading west on the dirt roads towards the little town of Apuela. The road peaked at a foggy 3400 metres and was well-made for rural Ecuador, meaning it was a one-lane wide road and mostly hardpacked. Still, neither Amy nor Timbit cared for it. Amy was not fond of the steep, uphill, off-camber hairpin turns, and Timbit dragged her poor little belly over all of the big rocks. By late afternoon we came across a large crew working on clearing one of the many landslides that covered the road on the westerly slopes. These work crews weren't like in North America with sun burnt flag people decked out in fluorescent vests. Here, we approached the machines and honked. They turned the machines to see who was there and stopped momentarily to let us by. It was up to us to quickly pick the best way through all the trees, mud, and debris that covered the road. We found out later that this road had only opened the previous day and had been closed since February. To have reached that section and be forced to turn around could have very likely sparked a mutiny from Amy, as I assumed the road was open and never bothered asking anybody to confirm that it was.

Outside of Apuela, we came across a weathered wooden house and two yellow BMW F650s with UK plates parked in the grass out front. Since we ran into few other motorcycles on the road, our curiosity was sparked and we stopped to find out more. They belonged to a travelling

English couple who were visiting friends that lived at the shack. They invited us to stay for a few days, and we spent time poring over maps and trading information on road conditions and interesting places to visit. This type of travellers' exchange was most valuable to everyone, being both up-to-date and motorcycle-specific.

Amy was itching to leave after one day, while I was content to look at maps, talk about the road ahead, and drink coffee. It was a style and

started thousands of years ago as wildlife tracks, which evolved into walking and donkey tracks, then wagon tracks before being widened for modern vehicles. With little money for bridges or expensive construction work, the roads followed the land, despite the sometimes circuitous route that entailed. Switchbacks wound up to a hill's crest, then descended down the other side. Heavy trucks alternated endlessly between belching black diesel all the way up a hill and limping all the way down with

Impromptu travellers' meeting.

Rural roads.

pace that had worked well for me in the past, and I wondered if Amy was anxious to ride because she wanted to ride, or because she was less than thrilled with our grubby accommodations. I forgot that I had adjusted to the dusty side of the travelling life over many months, while she had only recently been thrown into it at the end of an international airplane flight.

In addition to the people and scenery that continuously interested us, I was also intrigued with the road itself. Many roads in these rural areas

smoking, burning brakes.

We avoided the Pan-American Highway wherever possible because it was the quickest way to get from A to B, and therefore packed with trucks and buses. However, we made an honorable exception for the segment that skirted Chimborazo (6268 metres or 20,565 ft), the highest volcano in Ecuador. Here the road itself peaked at 4380 metres (14,370 ft), so the terrain was nothing short of spectacular. I fell in love with the cold, dry weather and the rocky mix of barren grays and browns. There was little vegetation, but there were hardy little patches of purple wild-flowers and low woody scrub. The wind howled non-stop. We reluctantly dropped off the plateau and headed into the jungle that contained some of the headwaters of the Amazon River that flow more than 6000 kilometres (3700 miles) east through Brazil to the Atlantic Ocean.

As we lowered our elevation, indigenous groups worked rectangular fields of potatoes and coffee using terraced hillsides and superbly engineered Incan stone waterways for irrigation. Weathered and smiling faces appeared beneath the ubiquitous Ecuadorian accessory – the felt hat. Despite the elevation, cool weather and spitting skies, they appeared very comfortable in fashionable knee-length skirts and bright shawls for the ladies and trousers and jackets for the men, often made from alpaca or llama wool.

A fresh batch of chicha underway.

Once in the jungle of eastern Ecuador, I was anxious to try the local chicha, an alcoholic drink made from fermented corn that has been enjoyed in many parts of South America since the time of the Inca. In corn-free jungles, however, chicha is brewed a little differently: the woman chews, spits and stirs a mixture of yucca root over and over for several days, using her saliva to augment the process of fermentation. After three days fermenting in earthen jars it is as alcoholic as beer, stronger if left up to seven days. The consistency is like a stringy thin milkshake, and the taste is predictably bitter but refreshing. When drinking large glasses of chicha I discovered that it is helpful to keep the teeth relatively close together to sieve out the not-well-chewed strands of yucca root.

Southern Ecuador's mild road construction and muddy roads from steady rain limited our movement to first and second gears as we slipped and slid our way to the border with Peru. Once there, we avoided the busy paved roads and drove several hundred kilometres inland past rice fields and green shallow valleys before catching a road south. In addition to avoiding much of the heavy traffic, we skirted in and out of the magnificent Andes mountain chain, the longest in the terrestrial world.

On many days we rested in the early afternoon when our natural energy levels ebbed. Making coffee or grabbing a Coca-Cola (available absolutely everywhere) helped to revive our energy. So did coca leaves. Once the coca leaves' little hard stems were pinched off, we squished the leaves between our teeth and the insides of our cheeks, like chewing tobacco, except no chewing was involved. The leaves were often combined with the ashes of plants, banana peels, or potato to promote the separation of the leaf's active alkaloids. The swallowed juice inhibited feelings of fatigue, thirst, hunger, and altitude sickness in us, as it had for the local population for over 4000 years. Its reputation as the source of America's woes caused regular protests by the coca leaf farmers, but we only witnessed one personally. Farmers in a coca-growing area burned tires across the highway and created an inconvenient, but non-violent statement against the interference of the US government's War on Drugs on their farming choices. They asked me if anybody in America really expected them to stop growing coca, which they have been doing for thousands of years, only to fix a problem in America? It was America's problem, so they should deal with it there. One demonstrator told me that he could earn 150 Bolivian soles ($15) for a kilogram of coffee beans, but 600 soles ($176) for a kilogram of coca leaves. I accepted his figures cautiously, but his argument became more persuasive when he added the solid reference of being able to harvest the coca leaves three times a year versus once a year for coffee.

Heading south from the northern Peruvian city of Chachapoyas we spent a leisurely day travelling the narrow, hot, potholed canyon along-side the meandering Utcubamba River, which was gorgeously clear, sometimes green, sometimes blue.

Near the end of the day, the high temperature warning light lit up Amy's dashboard. I went over a checklist of possible causes in my head. Fuses ok? Yes. Enough fluid in the radiator? Yes. Radiator clean of debris? Fan working? Aha. The fan would not move freely when pushed. I walked to my bike to see if mine was the same, and mine twirled easily when spun. So there was the issue. So now what? Could I fix it? We stripped the bike and removed the motor.

I tried my best to get the fan apart to see what had seized inside and prevented it from turning, but failed even to crack open the outer housing. Our choices were to continue nine hours over several mountain passes to the next small town, or go back to Chachapoyas. The latter was the obvious decision. Amy coasted back down to our last town, where a kind hotelkeeper allowed us to store the bike in his chicken coop and some of our luggage inside the hotel. We took what we thought we would need in Chachapoyas and started the four-hour trip back north.

I settled into the internet café in Chachapoyas to ask the online community of F650 owners about my problem. The group confirmed my diagnosis as a bad fan motor and suggested that I go buy a new one, which would have been solid advice if I was within striking distance of a BMW dealer. Instead, I decided to learn everything about radiator fan motors: how they work, how to repair them, or how to modify other fans that might be able to do the same job. Unfortunately, it became clear that outright replacement would be the only reasonable option. On a whim I emailed Dan Walsh, who was in the USA visiting a friend. He agreed to bring the part back with him when he returned to Peru in a few weeks'

Coca leaf break.

Local cowboy.

Trying to fix the radiator fan motor with no success.

A boy is silhouetted by the fireworks tower.

time, so I bought the small motor online from a dealer in the USA and had it couriered to him.

It was at times like this that I was glad I was not a working man on a two-week vacation trying to hit all the highlights of Peru and watching the valuable moments of his vacation tick away while throwing money at FedEx to try to save it. Our unintentional plan of having more time than money was working for us again. We moved into the classroom of a local English school with the manager of the school and his grandmother. The move was both to save money and also to sink deeper into daily Peruvian life. I taught three teenage girls English from 8:15 p.m. to 9:15 p.m. Monday to Friday in exchange for a mattress in the classroom for Amy and me to sleep on. The biggest challenge with the arrangement was that during the week there were classes most evenings and we could not drag our mattress out until the classes were done at 10:30 p.m., way past our usual bedtime.

I loved this arrangement, but Amy was not as enthusiastic about our accommodation. It was my opinion that we needed to continue to save money where we could, and living at the school allowed us to do that. In addition to the lack of privacy and late bedtimes, Amy felt bad for the grandmother whose semi-private toilet we destroyed regularly as we both fought off a flu bug. When tensions arose between Amy and me, it normally started with the budget. Our funds were dropping more quickly than I had expected, and I had gotten used to living on less. I loved the challenge of seeing how far I could get my money to go. Breakfast at the market was always a fried egg sandwich and instant coffee that was cheap and delicious. Amy could handle that two or three times a week, but not much more.

I grudgingly agreed to check into a hotel, but I became less grumpy about the move when I realized that I could watch the winter Olympics on the television there. Dan returned to Peru and sent the small motor to us by bus. It arrived just in time to keep me and Amy from pulling each other's hair out. With our ability to move assured, our moods improved and we hightailed it back to where we stashed the bike. In fifteen minutes, Timbit was running like new.

We soon passed the location of the breakdown and climbed steadily to the top of the pass. We had left the morning warmth of the valley, and the road shrank down to a single lane. Farmers' treeless fields of short grasses were on both sides of the road, as were short volcanic rock walls that separated the properties. We crested the top of the pass at 3600 metres (11,000 ft) and gazed deep into the valley below and the twisting, Ama-

Mosaics made from coloured sawdust decorate the plaza in honor of the virgin saint of Chachapoyas.

zon-bound Marañón River that it contained. It was a jaw-dropping sight, and we would have lingered longer if it had been warmer. The grassy hill-tops beside us looked warm and fuzzy, but there was nothing warm and fuzzy about the road on the south side of the pass. The one-lane road was carved out of the side of the cliff, and its slow descent in elevation was clearly laid out as it followed the curves of all the mountains to our left. If we were to encounter another vehicle, we would need to back up and find a place that was nominally wider to allow the pass.

Since we did not have a reverse gear, we fervently hoped that the other driver would be so kind. As it turned out, we did not come across another car, truck, or bus that day.

Later that week we completed the ride into Cajamarca (population 125,000), the largest city we had yet been to in Peru. Our accommodation looked out over the famous main plaza where, almost exactly 451 years earlier, the Inca race effectively came to an end when its leader, Atahualpa, agreed that his people would convert to Christianity. (He was still garroted by the Spanish.)

I had always thought that the Inca had disappeared mysteriously, like the Maya civilization of Central America. As I read the details of the Spanish conquest over the Incan people, my sympathy landed on the Incan side.

When that book was finished, I started another on how the Inca rose to domination by conquering their neighbours during the 300 years leading up to the arrival of the Spanish. My sympathy turned to resignation. I wondered if I would ever encounter a culture that did not use violence to force its divinely-granted beliefs into the lives of those around them.

Backpackers, climbers and hikers have known about the staggering scenery in the mountains in Peru for years. To see it for ourselves, we took the back roads to get to the Cordilleras Negra and Blanca, mountain ranges within the Andes profile that contain hundreds of glaciers and feature Huascarán, Peru's highest mountain at 6768 metres (22,204 ft).

We left the busy Pan-American Highway at the coastal town of Santa. With full fuel tanks we turned east and followed the glacier-fed Santa

View of Llanganuco Lake from 4000 metres, on the way to the 4767 metre (15,640 ft) pass of Portachuelo de Llanganuco.

Amy heads toward 6768 metre (22,270 ft) Huascarán from the 4920 metre (14,750 ft) pass of Punta Olympica.

Mount Huascarán still faces us as we continue the zig-zag descent down into the Ulta valley.

River and the canyon that cradled it.

It was hot, and although there was a river running in the bottom of the gorge, it was surprisingly lifeless. The towering mountains on either side were devoid of any life, and merely existed as walls of heat absorbing rock. We passed the ruins of many towns that had attempted to make a living in this desolate area. Their era was difficult to judge, as the adobe style of building was still a current construction method. The only work that it appeared the valley could support was small-claim coal mining, evident in a young man we saw walking on the road, covered from head to toe in black soot, with only the whites of his eyes visible.

At 4:30 p.m., we started looking for a hotel for the night. At a small shop we learned that there were three hotels in the next town, fifteen minutes down the road, and there was even a festival underway. What luck! We arrived in the town of Huallanca around 6 p.m., glad to be done for the day.

Signs of the festival were everywhere, from the folks in costume to the drunken men sleeping on the benches. We pulled up on the short section of the main street that was paved, enjoying the absence of dust for a few

blocks, and stopped at the police station to ask for directions.

This excerpt is from my journal from that day.

"A policeman came towards us wearing crisp green pants with a bright white shirt. He was cleanly shaven except for his manicured moustache, and was carrying two large bottles of beer and a one-litre bottle of Inca Kola ("a favourite since 1935," says the label). He crept towards us, grinning wildly, moving his hands up to his chest and wiggling the bottles of beer at us as a child would do while saying, "Looook whaaaaat IIIIIII gotttt." He was quite drunk. He invited us in, placed his drinks down on the desk, and proceeded to explain that he was with the Peruvian police, and that this (insert sweeping arm movement) was his jurisdiction. He smelled very nice. As he told us about the hotels in the town, "There are three hotels in town," he said, his hands moving independently of each other, and his voice shooting between squeaky high and normal. He was careful to explain which landmarks the hotels were close to for our convenience. After handshakes we prepared to leave. "But," he continued, "there is a fiesta in town...much music and dancing (insert a little tap dancing here) so the hotels are all full. You have to go to Caras. It's 45 minutes away and only nine kilometres of dirt road (insert image of him holding onto imaginary handlebars and going over what appear to be very large imaginary bumps). After the nine kilometres it is all highway (insert image of him doing a wheelie)."

So off we went into the Cañon del Pato, famous for its 35 tunnels cut into the bedrock during building because the gorge was too narrow to use conventional construction techniques. In the darkness of the tunnels, Amy let me know that my taillight would sometimes go out. "That's

One of the 35 tunnels in the Cañon del Pato.

okay," I told her, "It matches my burnt-out headlight, and that hasn't worked since Mexico."

We arrived after sunset, and set up camp for a week to let Amy deal with a bad food bug and for me to deal with motorcycle maintenance.

A pebble had wedged itself between the frame of the motorcycle and the radiator. Constant vibration had eventually put a pinhole in the radiator, allowing the coolant to drip out. I whipped up a batch of J-B

Weld and coated the hole shut. The following week, I noticed that one of the two bolts that held the motorcycle's rear sub-frame on was missing. Actually, only the outer half of the bolt was missing, since it had sheared in two. When the extra fuel tanks were full, the bike carried 200 kilograms including my weight, a considerable amount to handle over the rough roads. We sought out a local welder and drilled out the old bolt and installed a new nut and bolt in its place. We were moving again in two hours, a time I considered quite respectable.

Repairing a broken frame bolt.

Motorcycle maintenance.

Peru's most famous tourist attraction is unquestionably Machu Picchu, but that's only for the unlucky tourists without motorcycles. For us two-wheeled visitors, the famous attractions start with the numerous mountain passes, and in particular a lonely mining road near the town of Huancavelica.

The road followed the winding way of an old train line up out of Huancavelica; the bridge trestles were long since overgrown with grass and the rails taken away. Tunnels into the mountains still acknowledged the mining history of the area. The Spanish were here in the 16th century exploiting the rich lodes of mercury used in the processing of silver ore.

We climbed quickly to over 4000 metres (13,123 ft). We were now on the highest continuous road in the world and would not drop below 4000 metres for another 150 kilometres. The immense scope of the valleys was hard to grasp – they stretched lazily from one mountain range on our left, across the road and to another mountain range on our right. There were patches of snow on the highest peaks, but with our many layers of

ABOVE: Broad 4000 metre valleys grace the high plains of Peru.

BELOW: 5059 metres above sea level, the highest drivable road in the New World.

clothing we were comfortably warm. From the short rock half-walls I could see on the valley floor, I gathered not everyone felt so comfortable around here. These shelters offered limited protection to the shepherds from the wind and fierce sun while their alpacas grazed.

As high as we were, the road was about to get higher. Fifty-five kilometres from Huancavelica we turned left onto a mine access road. The highest drivable pass in the new world was three kilometres away.

We puttered up to the official sign that signified 5059 metres (16,598 ft) above sea level and we took a celebratory rest. Our current position allowed us to look the mountains and peaks surrounding us in the eye, rather than scurry around at their feet. The dirt under us was crunchy and slightly compactable as a soil, but very little chose to live there. The short, stubby grass from the morning's broad valleys gave way to collections of tiny, yellow flowers and more isolated clumps of tufted short grass among the rocks. A quick hike for photographs confirmed that the fuel-injected bikes worked much better at 5000 metres than I did.

The absence of anybody else at our spot enhanced the quality of our experience. There was no formal bus routing on this spur road, and apart from one passing dump truck we had the place to ourselves.

Where the buses do not go, neither do the tourists: chalk another one up for the benefits of motorcycles. We descended from our detour and although we had been travelling downhill for

I traded this woman my last bag of coca leaves for this photo, which was the only one I could take before my batteries died.

kilometres, we were still at over 4500 metres. I fell in love with this road because it was not a zigzagging switchback road up to a pass with an all-too-speedy descent on the other side.

Normally much of our mountain driving time was spent winding around the bases of mountains with occasional forays up and over them. Our current road allowed sufficient time at high altitude for the scenery to settle in, and observations to be pondered.

The lack of pollution made the outlines of the mountains razor-sharp against the blue sky, which was darker than usual from the elevation. The wind smelled of snow, but there were few clouds in sight.

The altitude did not keep herdsmen from starting villages in this tough-love land. The village of Santa Ines (4650 metres) was a collection of a dozen buildings on either side of the road, containing, of course, a small restaurant. Stopping for lunch or coffee at these small family-run cafés always pleased me. We would walk into a concrete block house to be greeted by long wooden tables, white plastic chairs, and posters of old movie stars on the walls, which were somehow always painted blue.

Plastic thermoses of hot water and glass jars of instant coffee crystals would appear, and we would warm our hands holding the thin tea-cups. Our dirty appearance did not bother the locals, and conversations quickly touched on where we were from and how we enjoyed their country. The laughing women in the kitchen and quiet conversations from old farmhands at a corner table made me want to ride every day in the cold and wind, just so I could warm up my hands on another cup with new friends in the next town.

Days of gradual downhill roads brought us to Cusco and a hotel that harboured five other motorcycle travellers whom we had met in the

The festival of huarachicoy, the Incan manhood rite, is reenacted at the walled fortress of Sacsayhuaman.

High passes are not always sunny. Amy tries to stay warm after a snowstorm.

previous few weeks. Many of the motorcycle overland travellers started to bump together with increasing frequency as we all attempted to arrive at the southern tip of Argentina for Christmas, when the weather was most bearable. We ended up leap-frogging each other and if someone found a beautiful road or cheap hotel with parking, an email went out to let the rest of the group know about it.

One of these suggestions was Colca Canyon, a wickedly deep gorge interesting in its own right, but special in the fact that it was the home of the Andean condor. The viewing was best in the early morning or the late afternoon and we gambled on arriving at the lookout area near sundown to ask the guard politely if we could camp next to the canyon.

The guard agreed and we set up camp and started the kettle. At 3800 metres, the temperature dropped as soon as the sun went down at 6:30 p.m., and we kept warm over pots of watery soup before crawling into the tent to stay warm and wait for sunrise.

The next morning, we wore all our clothes as we watched the sun come up, slowly heating the walls on the opposite side of the canyon. We packed and drank coffee while the tour buses arrived, and shortly after 8 a.m., the slow circling of the massive condors could be seen. They would stumble ungracefully out of the nest and spread their wings to catch the morning's rising air. We sat with our backs to the sun, growing warm in our heavy motorcycle clothes, and watched the birds reach the edge of the canyon where they passed closely by us, looping a half dozen times ever higher before they drifted out of view.

A quick and easy border crossing into Bolivia got us to the nearby town of Copacabana on the shores

Fresh and plastic flowers decorate motorcycles that stand in line to receive blessings from the monk at the Basilica of Our Lady of Copacabana.

of Lake Titicaca, often touted by the guide books as the world's highest navigable lake at 3812 metres (12,464 ft) above sea level.

It was a light-hearted town, popular with the tourists for its sandy beaches and its really slow boats to the Island of the Sun where, according to Incan legend, the sun god placed his representatives on earth and went on to develop the entire Inca culture. It was an easy day trip for Amy and me, and our time on the island allowed us to broach an unpleasant topic.

The previous weeks had seen a slow but perceptible rise in irritability between us. I found myself reminiscing fondly of my solo days. I found it difficult to go from travelling alone in Central America to being mechanic, boyfriend, translator, and tour guide. Months earlier I caught onto the fact that the ability to speak the local language infinitely increased the quality of the trip. Back then, I was forced to practise my Spanish at every

conversation, instead of speaking English most of the day as was the case now that we were a pair. I was seeing this and other trade-offs of travelling as two rather than one, and I was doubting my decision about that.

This is not to suggest that there were no benefits to travelling as a team. Having another set of hands and pair of eyes increases security, but that's not the top of the list. The greatest reward for travelling as a team is having a partner to participate in this significant event and the opportunity to reminisce about it afterward. It's the ability to sit years later and start conversations with "Remember when...?" Or, "I saw a guy today who looked identical to that guy who fixed your tire in La Paz. What was the name of the restaurant next door to there – the one with that soup you loved?"

Good memories are worth sharing, and that is most easily done with someone who was there with you.

Outside of the world's highest capital city of La Paz was the World's Most Dangerous Road, so called because of the number of deaths and accidents on it. It was a narrow route that dropped 3200 metres in less than 70 kilometres, offering all conditions from blowing snow to steamy green jungle. The slippery-when-wet surface, the instability of the surrounding hillsides, and the steep roadside drop-off didn't help the safety record. Accidents caused by tired truckers and poorly maintained vehicles added to the road's dark reputation.

It was the fact that the road was one lane wide but filled with two-way traffic that created most of the problems. When oncoming vehicles met at a narrow section of road (which is most of it) they had two options.

Amy sticks to the inside of the World's Most Dangerous Road.

The first was for one of the vehicles to back up to a location on the road that was wide enough to allow a pass. Unfortunately, putting any vehicle into reverse is a terrible blow to the machismo of Latino drivers, many of whom took their chances with the second option; creeping by each other and hoping for the best. The majority of deaths were due to drivers' underestimation of the location of their tires on the road, so much so that the local driving laws instructed drivers to keep to their left on this road. Now, a glance out of the window made downhill drivers aware of how close their tires were to the sheer drop that accompanies most of the ride. With the completion of an alternate route in 1996, the most dangerous part of this road may now be the hordes of tourists with rented mountain bikes who come to coast down the length of the road as part of an adventure outing.

We left our hotel in La Paz with one of the eight motorcyclists who also happened to be staying there. Tony, an Englishman on a Kawasaki KLR650, was travelling alone and when he heard of our plans to negotiate the remote roads, massive saltpans, and hot springs of the border area between Bolivia and Chile, he asked to join us.

We started our tour with a stop in Sajama National Park, home of Bolivia's highest volcano (6542 metres or 21,463 ft) of the same name. After an 11-kilometre sand road to the village of Sajama, we continued north for another seven kilometres to the signed turnoff of the first of our hot spring destinations. A warm, wide stream thwarted the path to our proposed campsite. It was less than knee deep, but full of melon-sized slimy rocks.

I crossed first and was promptly bucked off my bike after hitting one of the slimy melons. I picked up the motorcycle and a metre later, with wet gloves slipping on the clutch and throttle, I hit another rock and promptly dumped the BMW on the other side. I had dropped my bike only four times since the trip started, and two of them were in this sulfuric little stream. Since I was soaked to the knees, I went back and rode Amy's bike over without incident and then Tony's, too. We stopped in a sandy lot behind a mud-brick wall and hurried to set up camp. I was anxious to get out of my wet clothes since we were somewhere near 4300 metres (13,000 ft) and with the sun setting, the night's cold came quickly. We spent two days there, soaking and relaxing, watching the wandering herds of llamas foraging in our flat valley. Low overnight temperatures froze our water containers solid, but the sun was up by 6 a.m., by 7 a.m. it was warm, and by 8 a.m. it was hot, though the temperature was kept in check by a steady wind.

Sunset on Mount Sajama.

We crossed into Chile and were treated to flamingo-filled lakes and smoldering, snow-covered volcanoes under blue skies that made for a sublime afternoon ride.

We dropped 1000 metres into the small, warm town of Putre to ready ourselves for the upcoming trip south. Salar is the Spanish word for a salt flat, and we were on our way to see three of them, including the largest in the world, the Salar de Uyuni. We met a bicycle traveller in town who gave us a photocopied, hand-drawn map that he had received months earlier from another biker. The map had ridden up and down this lonely road multiple times with more information being added to it with each pass. I appreciated this greatly, as the government maps that we found had inconsistent data along this historically disputed border. Along with the distances, the map also noted smaller salars, hot springs and good camping sites, all useful details to have.

Other than the occasional mining truck coming north, there was nothing to disturb our 100-kilometre ride on the dirt road to the first salar, flanked by rolling scrubby hills. A smoking volcano was almost always visible from somewhere along the route.

Our first sight of the Salar de Surire was that of a glistening white lake, and we stopped at the ranger station at the north end of the salar to let him know that we would be camping there. He recommended we camp at the hot springs themselves, and kindly topped up our water supplies. The hot springs were across the lake from the ranger station, but we quickly found that the immediate shoreline was too soft to drive on. We moved to firmer ground around the perimeter of the lake, enjoying the flocks of pink flamingos and llama-like vicuñas prancing about.

We found the hot springs and set up camp behind a man-made rock wall and a tipped-over picnic table as the wind continued to howl off the surrounding mountains. We soaked the dust off and sank our toes deep into the black mud that made up the bottom of the pond. The cold nights meant a quick run in the morning across the frosty ground from the warm sleeping bag to the hot water. Breakfasts during cold weather often meant hard-boiled eggs were on the menu. When the eggs were cooked, we carefully pulled them out of the hot water and placed any extras in our inside jacket pockets to

Amy deals with the cool nighttime temperatures.

keep our bodies warm, as they held their heat very well and would make a delicious lunch later on. The leftover boiled water became coffee.

Cold mornings and riding in cold weather also had practical benefits for packing. When we wore most of our clothing to ward off the cold, it left plenty of space for packing the rest of our gear. However, the multiple layers of clothes took up any room under the motorcycle jacket and pants and gave us the awkward mobility of an astronaut in a space suit, which wasn't helped by our cargo of hardboiled eggs.

Our planned off-road route back to Bolivia and the other salars was eliminated after we encountered a DANGER MINES IN AREA sign and

Local flamingos enjoy a sunrise over their thermal pools.

a pile of barbed wire blocking the road. The next choice was a wonderfully bad dirt road that took us over a gently peaked 4800 metre (15,748 ft) pass. As we descended into the next valley, multiple roads branched off into the distance. Aiming to cross the valley as directly as possible, we followed the hand-drawn map as best we could, crossing shallow rivers and wide-open sandy plains. We saw nobody else the rest of the day. This, I imagined, was what Mongolia was going to be like: endless grass valleys and plains, making our own roads, and camping wherever we felt like it. A group of rheas – large, flightless birds similar to ostriches – running beside us brought my thoughts back to South America, and a few wrong turns later, we arrived at the Bolivian border.

Following the paved road from the border we ran into our first immigration stop, whose attendants were more interested in the motorcycles than any sort of immigration infraction. While we were there we pried directions from them to our next salar, the Salar de Coipasa. Their very general directions got us to the sandy turnoff heading south towards the dry lake. The next two miles were deep rutted sand and it was in our favor that the road dropped steadily in elevation from the paved road to the salar, as going uphill on that road with our smooth tires would have been a nightmare.

We never got a chance to ride in the middle of the Salar de Surire, so our first experience riding in the middle of the salt flats would be here on the Salar de Coipasa. Distant mountains shimmered on the horizon 44 kilometres away, while to my right the saltpan reached out forever. There it mixed with the blue sky and got caught up in the reflections of the clouds, blurring the separation between earth and sky. It was hard to imagine you were moving at all, until you looked down and saw the ground speeding past, and felt the odd salt crystal hitting you in the face, occasionally going in your mouth. Even as the horizon came into view, it lingered an extraordinarily long time before it was free of wavy heat lines, and even longer still before we found the road to the shore and were back on black, solid earthy dirt. We stopped to laugh at each other and let our eyes re-adjust to colours other than white.

Salar fun.

We consulted our four maps and the GPS to try to figure out the best way to get from where we were to the next town and re-fuel. On the maps, the routes always looked easy: wind around this mountain, go for a bit, find the town, have a beer. That five-hour, first-gear, sandy slog had the worst roads that wound around and around to all the little farms and one-horse villages and back on themselves before reaching our destination. Once we arrived, we realized there was a new road a mile or so away from where we exited the salar that would have taken hours off the ride. We arrived in the town too late to continue further and checked into the only hotel in town, which had rooms consisting of two beds crammed into a tiny space.

We parked the motorcycles in the hotel owner's grandmother's garden on the next block. During my entire stay in Latin America, the motorcycle was never parked on the street unsupervised. There was always a

spare room, kitchen, or guarded car park where the bikes could safely stay. Often this was at the insistence of the hotel. We were guests in their country, and our hosts wanted no misfortune to fall upon us. Awkward parking spots made me appreciate the relative lightness of our bikes compared to some of the big touring models we had seen on the road. Two years earlier my ego had taken a hit when I sold my large, manly 1150 to get the 650. Now, with 50,000 kilometres of experience and nobody around to impress with any fancy gear, I was extremely content with my decision. In addition to the ease of parking, my fuel economy was 26

Amy and Tony on the salt.

kilometres per litre of fuel. My less expensive bike also meant less money being tied up with the carnet and more money available for travelling. I also came to believe that a traveller's packing list grew to match the carrying capacity of the motorcycle; bigger bikes meant more stuff. Finally, I realized I would rarely be able to use the extra power of a larger bike. I

Getting fresh salt for the evening's pasta.

I had been thinking about camping on the salar for several weeks, and I had no trouble convincing Amy and Tony to join in. We selected a spot by pulling in the clutch and where we stopped, we set up camp. We had been warned about the cold, being nearly out of sight of any land and high (3650 metres, 11,975 ft). I played the guitar and hollered away as the sun dropped, draping us in a massive pink and red glow before slipping behind the horizon. After dinner we each took a spot away from the others and lay out on the salt watching the stars, listening for any noises. My ears buzzed from the lack of sound. There was complete silence, and I felt a tremendous sense of personal accomplishment at having come this far.

In the morning, the salt demanded more investigation. It dried in consistent but not identical patterns. I saw shapes with five, six, seven, and eight sides. It was a 10,000 km² hopscotch field with no toilet, which made me wonder about having to go for a squat on the salar. In addition to not having a bush, rock or anything else to crouch behind, the surface was too hard to dig a cathole, and any shit left on the dazzling white surface would probably be visible from space.

Nightfall on our salar campsite.

drove slowly because the roads were new to me and often I shared them with animals – most alive, some dead. After all, why rush?

By noon the next day we were at the edge of the Salar de Uyuni and the 10 billion tons of salt it contained. The shoreline of the salar itself was mucky, so we kept to the established tracks that led from the shore out to the solid salt centre. There was a proper rock and soil island in the middle of the salar which was our first stop. I programmed the GPS coordinates and hit the "go to" button. A big arrow flashed back at me pointing in a southwest direction, and we started the 42.8 kilometre countdown towards something nobody could see yet. We accelerated through the gears and settled on a conservative 80 kph despite the lack of speed limits. I preferred not to ride fast during these magical moments. I knew they would be over soon enough and I wanted to soak in all the details of the ride. As an experiment, I closed my eyes to see how long I could manage to drive at 100 kph without looking, but it was not long.

Around the edge of the salt shapes, a 1/2" high salt border separated one shape from its neighbour. It was the crushing of these borders that made the driving roads on the salar noticeable, and differentiated it from the rest of the untravelled area. The solid driving surface allowed trucks to transport goods quickly and directly across the dry lake instead of using the bad dirt roads around it.

A week after the salar, we descended into Sucre with our noses burned and our lips cracked from our months at high altitude. Sucre was a wonderfully white, old colonial city located on the way to the jungle. Its lower elevation meant pleasant weather, and we were happy to be able to wear only t-shirts at night again after the long time spent on the high plains. Through the magic of email, we met up again with Oz and Jessica, a couple from the UK whom we first met in Peru. We were happy to find out Dan Walsh had managed to remain sober enough to make it down from Peru as well. Gert, the owner of Sucre's popular Joyride bar, told us all that the 'Caravana del Che' was happening the following weekend. This was a four day off-road route that followed the last days of Che Guevara; it usually catered to quads, but welcomed motorcycles as well. Dan declined because he wanted to focus his energy on beating the record number of pints consumed at one sitting at Gert's place (which he did – 17) and because he was coming down with typhoid fever. Oz, Jessica, Amy and I were eager to go. We bought cheap knobby tires and waited for the weekend to arrive.

With no riding or other crisis to keep us occupied, Amy and I had a minor meltdown. The last few days with Tony from the Salar de Uyuni to Sucre were through spectacular country, but Amy and I did not enjoy the riding. There was an uncomfortable tension, mostly generated by me. I felt increasingly drawn to travelling alone and was not able to keep my intentions inside. I was also aware that the trip had become more important to me than my relationship with Amy, but I couldn't think of any way to resolve that respectfully.

The rest of the week I spent with Tony in the hospital, as he had also come down with typhoid fever. I translated for the doctor and nurses and did supply runs to the pharmacy. The doctor gave me the prescription and I walked to the pharmacy to buy the syringes, little glass vials of painkillers, antibiotic pills, and bags of saline. I brought everything back to the hospital and registered them with the nurses to be administered later. I was proud to be able to get his insurance sorted, schedule an enema (for him), and get a CAT scan appointment. Since the CAT scan machine was at a different hospital and the ambulance was busy, I hired a taxi and put Tony with his revealing hospital gown in the front seat while I held his intravenous drip above him from the back.

My Spanish hospital vocabulary was improving, but unfortunately my lessons were not over yet.

The Caravana del Che started in the countryside, and after getting a map of the route and general directions, riders were free to go at their own speed. Our group of four kept together and was regularly passed by the faster quads and motorcycles. That was comforting only in the sense that we knew were on the right road. As Gert promised, the trail consisted of sections of off-road jeep track linked by steep, rocky sections, muddy jungle crossings, slick sandstone, and grassy knolls, all strung together with plenty of stops for beer and food. During regular travelling we never got the opportunity to ride our bikes with knobby tires and almost no luggage, and I had forgotten how fun motorbikes could be in the dirt when you were not carrying your house and all of your worldly belongings with you.

La Higuera is the small village where Che Guevara was executed

Memorial to Che Guevara in the town of his death, La Higuera.

on October 8, 1967. We rode up to the memorial in the afternoon to join the 100 people who had already arrived. I wondered if the celebration of Che's ideology was lost on some of those who were on the ride, as many people riding with us had accumulated great wealth through business and capitalism in Bolivia, things that Guevara detested.

We left the memorial after the obligatory photo and headed back up the valley to the top of the winding ridge where the main dirt road brought us to the campsite and party for that evening. Dinner featured four pigs split in half and roasted over an open fire, dutifully turned by local kids who spun two pigs each, one spit in each hand. Having one of the larger importers of alcohol into Bolivia on the ride had its perks, as all the drinks were free after 8:30 p.m., and the bands and DJs played well into the night. We learned new dances, all of which I have forgotten, and stumbled to bed way past our regular bedtime.

The camp was slow to rise the next morning, partly because of the previous night's debauchery and partly because we were on the last day of the tour and the route was flat, wide and relaxed.

The morning's roads were shaded and cool but the sun showed its strength when it crested the tops of the trees. As usual, Jessica and Oz were ahead, as they normally rode quicker than Amy and I. Twenty-one kilometres from the end of the ride I saw the back of Amy's motorcycle fishtail to the left and right. The bike went down, throwing Amy over the handlebars and sending up a plume of dust. I arrived in seconds, wondering why she was still down. Normally after a crash she bounced up and tried to erase any evidence that she had crashed by the time I got to her. Her right knee was giving her intense pain, and she knew that some-

Amy after her fall.

thing was badly wrong. Jess and Oz had circled back and we repositioned her so that she lay on the road with the damaged leg elevated and waited for the quads to arrive, hoping one had a radio. Her day was over. When the main group showed up, someone went to the next village to scrounge up some old lumber to use as a splint while a pickup truck arranged to take her to the next town of Samaipata for x-rays.

On the way there, my head was filled with "what to do next?" questions. That morning the plan had been to finish the caravana and take two days to head back to Sucre, then keep travelling with Jess and Oz to the Salar de Uyuni again. After that, we would exit to Argentina to meet my sister who was arriving with her backpack, and travel as a group of three. This was unlikely now.

In Samaipata we went to the local hospital for x-rays, but they did not have an x-ray machine, so the truck continued to the larger city of Santa Cruz, two hours to the east. Jess, Oz and I stayed behind to arrange for Amy's bike to get to Santa Cruz, and then followed her to the hospital. It was November 2, which was the Day of the Dead in many Latin American countries, and we passed cemeteries packed with well-dressed people bringing flowers and gifts to decorate the graves of loved ones.

When initial x-rays indicated more than just a strain or sprain, we formally checked into the hospital and got ready for a MRI the next morning. I was glad to be in a classier hospital than Typhoid Tony had had back in Sucre. The service and food were excellent, they let me sleep on the couch in the room with Amy, and I got free Q-tips. On our first night we watched CNN incredulously as George W. Bush was re-elected president of the USA and figured that if bad things do happen in threes, that third one was going to be particularly nasty.

Jessica and Oz checked on us every day, smuggling beer and Pringles into the room to cheer us (mostly me) up. Amy was depressed about her silly crash, as she was usually a very cautious rider. The MRI and subsequent x-rays showed a torn posterior cruciate ligament. After talking with Amy's insurance company and having a conference call with an American doctor and the surgeon from the Bolivian hospital, we scheduled arthroscopic surgery for Saturday night, which was then bumped to Sunday. After the two-hour surgery Amy was in considerable pain, and walking to the bathroom put tremendous pressure on her leg, so I learned the Spanish word for "bedpan" and a new skill for my resume. The following week I learned the Spanish word for "tampon."

We were anxious to find out what the recovery time was, but it was hard to nail down an answer. One doctor said that the screw that was put in could come out in six months; another said a year before walking. A third said three months without moving the leg, then three months before walking.

It was not an option for Amy to stay in Bolivia to recover, so we made plans to get her home to her parents' place in America. She flew home ten days after the surgery, and I sent her motorcycle the following week.

We checked in with each other as often as we could by email, and weekly by phone. She let me know that although her knee was painful, her heart hurt more. I felt terrible about how the trip had ended for her and how little I could do to help her recover. In a macabre way, the accident accelerated the timing of the decision to continue travelling together or not. Our relationship was already on precarious ground, and with my waning commitment to it and now a nine-month separation, I doubted it would survive.

Before Amy's crash, we had planned to meet my sister Brigitte in Salta, Argentina and drive as a group of three on the two bikes to the southern city of Ushuaia for Christmas. With Amy and her bike back in America, my options for travelling with Brigitte became more limited. It took two days for me to reach Brigitte's hotel in Salta, where we sacrificed all non-essential goods, including the camping gear and guitar, and mailed them to the post office in Ushuaia where they would be held for one month. She would get one of the rear aluminum panniers for her things and I would take the other. With the bike packed, Brigitte hopped on the back and we headed to the bottom of South America.

In order to make it to Ushuaia – a long way south on the archipelago of Tierra del Fuego – by December 25, we had to put in several long days.

The bigger car always wins.

Our second day was particularly bad. Northern Argentina was pampas country, wide swaths of grassland that was excellent for feeding massive herds of cattle, but there was little of interest for a slow motorcycle. It was ten hours in 40C heat through bleak, scrubby bush with straight, uneventful roads. As we pulled up to the hotel Brigitte was furious with me and got off the bike in a huff. At first I thought she was still angry with me for using her pen cap to clean my ears that morning, but it soon came

tos throughout the book and one aspect of the story was the learning of photography along the way.

With the production of future calendars and perhaps a book in mind, I bought a 7.2 megapixel Sony camera with almost twice the resolution of the old one, while my brother generously pitched in a MacBook computer to house all the photographs. I now had no excuses for blurry, out-of-focus, or lost pictures. I almost convinced myself that I also needed a compact, thin camera that I could take to dinner or the bar to capture those spontaneous moments. A moment of rationality – increasingly frequent these days – forced me to accept the fact that the bigger camera would do just fine for those moments; I simply needed to be less lazy about bringing it.

The Vancouver International Motorcycle Show was the last of the three shows and I rented a cargo van to bring the bike and myself there. This show was larger than the Calgary or Edmonton shows, but the site was 45 minutes east of downtown Vancouver. After long days of talking, I preferred to drive into a nearby town for a quiet beer before returning to the exhibition grounds parking lot to camp in the back of my empty van. In the mornings I prepared myself for another day by going to the municipal pool for a quick swim.

With the show finished, I took the boxes of leftover calendars to Vancouver bookshops and motorcycle shops to try my luck there. Part of the feedback I received, especially from the motorcycle shops, was that once people had picked the calendars up and looked through them, they would be stained with greasy fingerprints and not sellable. Based on that valuable advice, I bought a small vacuum food sealer and spent the next two weeks placing one 2006 and one 2007 calendar into a vacuum-sealed bag to keep them fresh for their new owners, which became fewer and fewer as spring approached.

Back in Edmonton, I tallied my receipts in anxious expectation, wondering how my selling venture had done. To my surprise, I had taken in $10,600. Visions of being able to travel for unlimited years without working danced in front of my eyes.

Then I added up the expense column: $14,900.

Oddly, I was happy with the fact I had not lost too much money, and I still had more than a thousand calendars to do something with.

My sister Brigitte and I thought door-to-door selling would be a good way to sell a hundred or so, and we drove to Fort Saskatchewan, the small town where we had grown up. We started on our old street, and at the end of a few hours of knocking on doors, Brigitte had sold two calendars and I had sold one. It was not the productive afternoon we had hoped for, but at least it was enough for gas money and ice cream.

With summer approaching, I crated the motorcycle and arranged to have it shipped by ocean to Johannesburg. I would meet it there in August of 2006 and start the next leg of the journey.

The day before the plane left, I had one last errand to complete. I returned to the used clothing donation centre and dropped off the pants and work shirts that I had purchased a year before, an act that gave me great satisfaction.

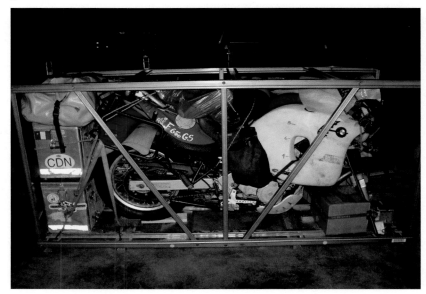

Strapped in and bound for Africa.

CHAPTER 5
AFRICA

While I was in South America, I received an email from Elroy and his wife Mandy, motorcyclists from South Africa who were following my travels on the web. They offered to host me in Johannesburg upon my arrival there, and I was not about to disregard such a warm invitation. I eagerly accepted and looked forward to meeting them in person.

Elroy picked me up at the airport and used the time on the drive home to explain road rules as they apply in Johannesburg. Lane splitting is legal, and speed limits are not normally adhered to. After midnight, red traffic lights and stop signs are only suggestions. There are speed cameras permanently mounted along roads, and you must slow down for them, but can speed up afterward.

Over dinner Mandy took over and offered a lesson in Afrikaans, the world's youngest language.

"You only need to know three words: 'Howzit', 'lekker', and 'robot'. 'Howzit' is a general greeting and is the shortened form of 'How is it?' The reply, of course is 'lekker', which means great. 'Robot' is our word for a traffic light. If you ask for directions and somebody tells you to turn right at the next robot, don't look for a shiny tin man."

I needed to finish a week of paperwork before Mandy and I could get the bike out of customs. An hour after the last stamp was placed on my forms, the bike was assembled in the parking lot and I was ready to follow Mandy home. I was grateful for her guidance, as this was the first time on the trip that I was driving on the left-hand side of the road. I kept Mandy firmly in sight as I relaxed and let the fact sink in that I was on my way to start the next leg of the journey.

"I'm riding a motorcycle in bloody Africa – I don't believe it," I murmured to myself. I let out an old-fashioned cowboy whoop while a delighted smile settled on my face.

After a day of running errands in Johannesburg traffic, I was comfortable with the left-hand driving. Following other vehicles was the easiest way not to screw up, and I made certain that I was never at the front of a line of cars, especially coming into a traffic circle.

With my new driving skills in place, I left some luggage with Mandy and Elroy and made a small, fast loop in the southeastern areas of Africa, returning to Johannesburg via Mozambique and Swaziland to prepare for the twelve-month long road north to Russia. A stack of maps and a pot of tea were all I needed to spend the day planning routes, one of my favourite parts of travelling. The majority of the planet's land mass is north of the equator, and this curious twist of geography presents some challenges for choosing a course that will avoid snowy winters and rainy seasons. I wanted to miss

Bad planning forces me to use the local gas station in Mozambique.

East Africa's rainy November and December, but I also wanted to stay well away from the scorching heat of summer in the Arabic Peninsula. Ideally, I would arrive in Russia and Mongolia sometime between the river-swelling snowmelt of spring and the freezing temperatures of winter.

As I prepared to leave Mandy and Elroy's home for the final time, I finished replying to emails that were piling up. A few people I had met at the motorcycle shows in Canada were contacting me and asking for advice regarding trips to South America. I was happy to give my two cents' worth and included the following tip: spend more time in the places that will be hardest to get back to again. As I hit the send button on the email, I realized I was about to ignore the same advice that I was giving out. Here I was in Africa – completely across the globe from my home – and I was anxious get through it in a few months. What was my hurry?

Some of the 10,000 virgins dancing for Swaziland's King Mswati III in the 2006 Umhlanga festival, where he will choose his 15th wife.

My initial plan had been to take four months to cross Africa from south to north. With a fresh pot of tea, I decided that it would be wiser to tour southern Africa while I waited for the weather to improve in the north. That increased my time in Africa from four months to at least nine. I did not know where the time or money for the extra travel was going to come from, but I didn't have to answer that question right away. Once I was on the Arabian Peninsula, I would have spring on my side, and from Iran I could ride the warm coattails of spring as it swept north, bringing me to the territories of Russia and Mongolia during the long days of the northern summer.

I set my immediate sights on Botswana and left for a final coffee with Elroy and his riding group.

At the coffee shop, I befriended a German man who was very interested in the motorcycle and the trip. As we finished our drinks and conversation, Klaus called his fiancée in Botswana's capital city of Gaborone where he lived, and asked if he could bring a guest home. She apparently said yes, because a few minutes later I had directions to the house.

Gaborone was on my way north and I welcomed the chance to see a new city with a local resident. I crossed the border in the afternoon, and after a lazy two-hour ride to get to the house, I arrived at a quaint wooden home in a quiet rural setting outside the noise and busyness of the city. The sliding gate opened and I entered along a short driveway past well-tended gardens of flowers and vegetables; the scene reminded me of the Swiss countryside.

I was introduced to the fiancée and a few minutes later they left for a previously arranged function, apologizing to me for the bad timing. Before they left, they told me that there was a pizza in the oven and beer in the refrigerator for me. A scalding hot shower and a cold beer had me good as new and I fell asleep on the couch waiting for my hosts to return. The next morning over strong coffee I discovered that my lady host was Unity Dow, Botswana's first female judge of the High Court and acclaimed novelist. We talked casually about Botswana and she gave me suggestions on what to see while I was there. When I explained the

upcoming day's route, I asked her advice on where to camp that evening.

"Mopipi," she replied. "It's a nice little town, and the people there are very friendly."

If the place was good enough for a Botswana High Court judge, it was certainly good enough for me.

It was a day of road construction and watery Kalahari desert horizons until the road sign advised me that Mopipi was ahead. On the left was a considerable saltpan and on the right was the upcoming mud brick town and its dusty roads. It was not a place I would normally choose for a night's rest. The highway ran alongside the town, and I was able to drive by the entire place before realizing there was no more to it, and turned around to find a place to camp. I needed that morning's encouragement from Justice Dow to stop and ask for a place to stay for the night.

I tried my luck at the gasoline station where I saw a potential place to put my tent. I went in to ask if it was possible for me to camp beside a nearby wooden fence.

Mopipi, Botswana.

BUY A N$ 3-00 TICKET AND STAND A CHANCE TO WIN A NEW CELL PHONE OR A BIG GOAT OR A TASTY FRIED CHICKEN FROM OVIKANGE PS - FUND RAISING COMPETITION DRAW. TICKET NO# 400
Name:
Place:
Cell:
GOOD LUCK!!

Fundraising draw for the local school.

"Sure, why not?" they replied.

"That was easy," I thought, and after setting up the tent went into the attached restaurant for a warm beer and a cold piece of fried chicken.

Four young women kept the place running smoothly; one to help fill gas, one on the cash register, and two in the kitchen. They had questions about Canada, I had questions about Botswana, and the customers coming in to buy fuel questioned why nobody was working the pump.

This kind of interchange is why motorcycle travel is so unique: it allows you to get to where the tourists are not, to places where the locals are as interested in you as you are in them. This cultural exchange of the most basic kind is harder to find and less authentic in places that have a heavy influx of transient tourists.

The motorcycle provides an easy starting point for questioning from the locals, usually starting with "How much does it cost?" This question can be embarrassing to answer in areas where the imbalance of wealth is so obvious. If the question is asked quickly at a red light or the gas station, I will joke that "This is not a motorcycle, it is my wife, and she is not for sale." Most often that dissolves the question, but not for the man who suggested that we should trade wives because he liked mine better.

Before heading south to my eventual destination of Cape Town, South Africa, I continued northwest in northern Namibia to the border with Angola and the much talked about Epupa Falls.

I was disappointed with the falls because crocodiles prevented me from sinking my hot and dirty bones for hours in the Kunene River. There was little point in my sticking around a dusty campground if the river was off-limits. I left after one night and headed south on the well-graded roads. Namibia's dirt roads are maintained by graders who are paid for

Himba girls of Northern Namibia.

🎓 THE UNIVERSITY OF GRAVEL ROADS

each kilometre they complete, and tow a trailer behind the grader which they use for sleeping in whenever their work for the day ends.

A wide, dry riverbed thirty minutes south of the falls made me sweat as the bike powered and plowed its way through the thick river sand. The sarcastically named Good Road Bar was on the south side of the dry riverbed and became my temporary home as I waited out the heat of the day and watched the 4x4s crawling north to visit where I had just came from.

Unbelievably, this area is known as grazing country, and the nomadic pastoralist Himba people walk here with herds of drought-resistant cattle, sheep and goats. From the goats, they make leather for their loincloths, and they colour their skins with red ochre and fat to help protect them from the sun. Water is reserved for the cattle and rarely used for personal hygiene. The colour of their skin is striking, and shines beautifully in the afternoon sun.

At a campsite one night, I met Sidney from Cape Town who was riding a KTM. Sidney was a computer guy and quite comfortable sleeping in lodges on his tours. Since we were both heading towards the coast the next day, I convinced him that it would be fun to bush camp in the wild the next night. First thing in the morning, we stocked up on meat and alcohol for the evening's meal.

We bumbled along a seldom-used but well-maintained dirt road towards the coast, keeping our eyes open for a nice sheltered spot to set up camp. Sidney's eagerness to sleep in the desert waned as the day went on, and he was much fussier about the location of our camp than I, so by 4 p.m. we still had not come to any agreement as to where would be a good place to spend the night. We were about 60 kilometres from the Namibian coast and Sidney now felt we should push on into dusk and camp at the seaside.

I reluctantly agreed, and we sped closer to the coast, leaving our warm blue desert sky and sliding into a cold, evil, grey coastal air system. The current along this coast comes up from Antarctica and although it's awful for swimming, the fishing is great.

We arrived at the Mile 108 fishing camp at dusk and inquired at the small office for a campsite and a couple of Cokes.

"No problem with the campsite, but I'm afraid we are out of Coke," the office guy replied.

"How is that possible?" I asked, incredulous. "Africa runs on Coke! Nobody is ever out of Coke."

"We had some, but those South Africans in the big tent took them all." He motioned toward the shore, where a monster canvas tent like they used to have on M*A*S*H was set up.

I glared towards at the tent, and thought to myself, "Those bloody South Africans!"

My grumpy thoughts were interrupted by a man introducing himself. "Hi guys, I'm BJ. Get settled and then come to the tent for a beer."

"Hey," I changed my mind. "These South Africans are all right!"

We took the bikes and started toward a spot down the beach, but a red-moustached man with a huge smile stopped Sidney in front of the canvas tent. He came out with beers and introduced himself as Henk. He was with a large group from Cape Town on an annual fishing trip and within two minutes of the beers being opened, it was decided that we were their guests for the night and there was to be no arguing about it.

I stayed for another day and learned how to surf cast while Sidney drove back to South Africa. Before I said goodbye to my new camping friends, Henk gave me the GPS coordinates for his farm near Cape Town and insisted I stop by and visit if I made it down. It was nice to have a friendly contact in a new place and it gave me a slight feeling of coming home, even though I had never been there.

South of Mile 108, the coastal road is a salt road, which is made by mixing compacted sand with gypsum and salt water. When the road is dry, the traction is very good and the surface is hard as asphalt.

I plodded along the coast until the road ran into Swakopmund, a town now centred on the tourist experience and re-branding itself from a stodgy turn-of-the-last-century German port to a modern adventure capital. Skydiving, sand-dune sledding, and quad biking outfits littered every corner.

Namibia's most dramatic geographic features are the sand dunes at Sousesvlei.

for a job for the upcoming six months while the rains ran their course in eastern Africa. I had no idea what to do and since I had only a tourist visa, any work I could get would be technically illegal.

My stay was made easier after visiting Henk, when he offered me the chance to stay in one of the little wooden houses a hundred metres from the main house on his apple farm. If there was ever a perfect place to

Natural hazards of Namibian roads.

Like the Patagonian area of South America, Namibia's population density is among the world's lowest. This has superb consequences if one enjoys camping in the wild and discovering quiet back roads. In fact, the drive from the northern river border with Angola to the southern river border with South Africa can be completed almost entirely on gravel roads. Early colonization by Germany and subsequent administration by South Africa helped to develop a country with a strong infrastructure, which in turn attracted tourists who wanted an authentic African desert and wildlife experience, but who also placed value in safety, sausages, and good beer.

I arrived in beautiful Cape Town at the end of September. It's a liberal city that was easy for me to enjoy, reminding me of Vancouver in both lifestyle and natural environment. My first task upon arriving was to look

spend time, it was there, 80 kilometres east of Cape Town. A one-room wooden cottage with a toilet, shower, double bed and electricity made up the living area, and another wooden cottage of a similar size had a two-burner gas range, a compact refrigerator and a kitchen sink. The small patio faced southwest over acres of rolling hills, apple trees and vineyards in the distance.

Henk kept busy with farm details and new or existing tourism projects. A veteran of hundreds of trips to Namibia, he would drop all the daily farm jobs for a chance to get up there to deliver a part to one of the Zulu Overland tourist trucks that he owned, preferring his motorcycle as his delivery vehicle. His wife Maryke is a woman of infinite patience who has seen hundreds of Henk's ideas come and go over the years. With a catering business that was running at full steam, she had no time to worry about Henk, but she didn't really need to anyway.

On occasion, I went with Henk and Maryke to cater events. Henk was clever enough not to get in Maryke's way with any of the details of the catering, with the exception of making the fire and tending to the spit roasting – two activities which come naturally to all South African men.

While Henk watched the meat, my role was to keep his double brandy and Coke topped up. Admittedly, I was not an exemplary employee, as I often got sidetracked talking to guests about South Africa or motorcycles.

At a neighbour's 40th birthday party, Maryke, Henk and I attended to the catering. In between trips to the bar for Henk, I got involved in a heated debate with an attractive brunette about the old wives' tale regarding "things happening for a reason." Colette said things certainly do happen for a reason, and I argued that they most certainly do not. In my view, things just happen, yet humans are very good at making connections and plopping cause-and-effect relationships where there shouldn't be any.

Before I could get any deeper into the argument, I was pulled away by the sight of Henk staring at me and meaningfully tipping his glass upside-down. But I had managed to find out where Colette worked and I told her I would stop by and visit the following week. As the night wound down, I got another contact, this time on the travelling side. The neighbours had a niece who had travelled through Africa on a BMW with her husband; the pair were now stationed in Dubai, taking a break from their travels to earn some money. I took down their email address and made a note to ask them for any advice for the way up Africa or across the Arabian Peninsula.

Four days later, I arrived at Colette's work. I met her with a friendly handshake and told her I had a full day planned for us on the motorcycle. It became clear that she hadn't been awaiting my arrival with breathless anticipation when she asked, "What was your name again?"

I was startled but managed to stammer out, "Rene."

"Oh, that's right. I should have remembered that, since it's the same name as my brother," she said with a laugh.

"Yes," I thought. "You should have."

I was tempted to throw out a snotty "Everything happens for a reason," but I resisted the urge, and soon we were both on the BMW taking a slow coastal breakfast run in search of calving southern right whales. It was hard to not have an impressive day when the morning ride by the ocean transitioned into an afternoon of gorgeous vineyards and a picnic of local wine and cheese on a nearby mountain pass. This was certainly the television commercial version of adventure travel by motorcycle. The idyllic commercial would not go on to show the moment when, after two dates, you get a raised eyebrow and the question "Didn't you wear that last time we went out?"

The courting period available to a travelling motorcyclist with only two sets of clothing can be quite short.

By January of 2007, Colette and I were spending most of our days together, choosing to remain blissfully ignorant about what was going to happen in a few months when I left. January also meant calendar selling season in Canada, so my sister and brother contacted the motorcycle shows in Calgary and Edmonton and were allowed to sell the 2007 version of the calendars on my behalf. I needed them to sell $3500 worth in order for me to break even on the printing and expenses of selling the calendars. I was extremely grateful when the email came advising me that they had taken in $2200. I had lost a little bit of money on the calendar exercise, but I had enjoyed writing and putting it together, and I started thinking about another one for 2008. I was determined to be able to break even on a project like this and tell my story in a fun way at the same time. Having this plan forced me to take more photos from the road and take more detailed notes about the places I went.

By April, I had ridden countless miles with the hardcore local motorcycle clubs and toured the very best roads that South Africa had to offer. April was also the time for me to leave. Colette and I spent our final weekend together visiting small towns on South Africa's sparsely populat-

The infamous Sani pass from foggy South Africa to the mountaintop kingdom of Lesotho.

ed west coast. We had no concrete plans for what to do with our relationship moving forward. She did not ask to join the trip and I did not invite her. This was a solo trip, a truth confirmed for me in South America. We simply agreed to stay in touch and see what happened next.

I hurried back through Namibia, Botswana, and into Zambia, where I was anxious to see Victoria Falls by the light of a full moon. At the falls the Zambezi River drops 100 metres into the gorge below, sending up spray as high as 400 metres. When the moon is full and the skies are

THE UNIVERSITY OF GRAVEL ROADS

clear, the light from the moon creates a rainbow in the rising mist, and I added moon rainbows as another entry into my journal of things that I have experienced that I didn't even know existed before the trip started.

I started to use the appearance of a full moon to give me an excuse to go somewhere or do something that I would not normally do, as I felt the celebration of the full moon was a noble one. Since my travelling schedule was slower than most, the full moon was also a convenient gauge of passing time, and rarely was I able to spend two of them in one country.

This 30-second exposure catches the moon-powered rainbow over Victoria Falls.

Elephant speed bumps.

Rural Malawi shops.

Using a back way to Zambia's South Luangwa National Park, I underestimated (again) how long it would take me to complete the 120 kilometres of trail. I was still 80 kilometres short of my destination village when the sun set at 6 p.m., and I didn't want to bush camp in the national park, so when I stumbled into an anti-poacher ranger camp, I asked to spend the night. Two groups of five rangers take turns doing a 10-day, 110-kilometre tour of the park to try to combat poachers of ivory and bush meat. The poachers often use wire leg snares to disable their prey for days until they can kill it. Ironically, electric wires donated by well-meaning NGOs to protect villages from elephants are stolen by the killers to make these snares. The 120-kilometre distance I had to cover would eventually take me 10 hours.

After a quick tour of southern Malawi, I set up camp on the southern end of Lake Malawi. I fell into a groove that had me quite content to relax on the beach and send text messages to Colette telling her of my experiences in short, misspelled sentences.

Near my tent were Guy and Marleen, an extensively-travelled Belgian couple whom I had met briefly in Cape Town and who were heading north with their camperized 4x4 truck. To pass time, we speculated on upcoming roads and talked through what we thought routes to the north would be like. All roads appeared fun when you looked at them on a map with a cold beer in your hand.

However, there was one road that did not get any better-looking, no matter how much I drank, and that was the Lake Turkana route from Kenya to Ethiopia.

Traditionally, travellers going from Kenya to Ethiopia had two options: the main (bad) dirt road north from Nairobi, or a little-used (really bad) road through the remote northwest section of the country near Lake Turkana. It was little used because it was 900 kilometres between fuel stops through remote desert country on bad doubletrack. Guy had his sights set on this route and suggested that it would be fun if I came along. I told him I would consider it and went back to my other current favourite pastime, which was making bread.

For three weeks, I experimented with yeast and flour and finding the

Boys on the side of the road hold up skewered field mice as a delicacy to passing cars. The mice are boiled, and after the bitter intestines are removed, toasted in the fire. Ten for $0.70.

Campfire banana bread.

correct time that the dough needed to rise. My oven was a narrow rock-lined hole in the sand. On the bottom went hot coals from my fire, then a few spacer rocks, and then a CD-sized piece of wire mesh that I had found in a ditch. My titanium pot was terrible at dissipating heat, so the temperature below it needed to be low but consistent; I found that small embers placed alongside the pot helped to keep a steady heat, and coals heaped on the closed lid helped to cook the bread from the top. After thirty minutes, I occasionally had a spectacularly golden-brown fluffy loaf of bread that I proudly doled out to my neighbours. More often than not, I had a failed experiment that I ate alone.

On the way north through Malawi, my South African motorcycle friends advised me by email that movie stars/motorcycle adventurers Ewan McGregor and Charley Boorman were coming my way as they completed a drive from Scotland to South Africa for their documentary *The Long Way Down*. I was hoping to pilfer their parts car, but never did come across their sizeable entourage on the road.

I stopped to visit some hot springs along the shore, and the host of the campsite there confirmed the passing of the television crew and that

I had missed them by a day. Unbothered by missing my chance to pick up free tires, I headed off to the hot springs, but African hot springs are working hot springs, and a lineup of women with laundry took up most of the room near the waters' source. There was no room for a quick skinny-dip in these pools.

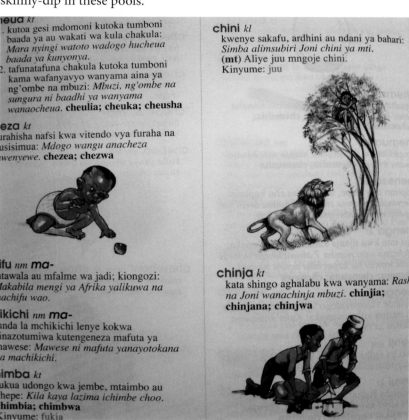

An illustrated children's dictionary shows Swahili words and pictures not normally found in English children's books.

I finished the border formalities to exit Malawi and drove the short distance to the entry post of Tanzania, where I greeted the customs officer with the polite greeting in Chichewa, Malawi's language. The officer

returned the greeting in Swahili and then in English.

The number of times the language changed in Africa was one of the conditions that made it more difficult to sink my tires deeper into the local culture. As soon as I learned how to say hello, goodbye, please, thank you, and beer in the local dialect, another week of travel brought me to an area where the dialect or language changed and the language lessons started all over again. My thirteen-country route through southern and eastern Africa exposed me to twenty official languages, eighteen recognized non-official languages, and hundreds of indigenous dialects. Fortunately for me, English was spoken at least a bit in most places. Between my handy traveller's sign language, the locals' broken English, and my ten hastily-acquired words in the local language, I could make my basic needs understood. As easy as the day-to-day living was, however, I longed for the gradual progression of comprehension that I had developed in South America by practising Spanish daily over the course of months, and the quality of conversations that came along with that.

LEFT: Wataturu family, western Tanzania.

ABOVE TOP: Signage reminding locals not to take the law into their own hands.

ABOVE BOTTOM: My regular breakfast restaurant featuring chapati, delicious unleavened bread cooked on a skillet.

for so long, we had trouble adjusting to the oncoming traffic. Not only because we were used to having the whole track to ourselves, but also because in Ethiopia they drive on the right-hand side of the road – my first African country to do so. Our first camp in Ethiopia was heavily laced with cold beer from a local bar. We happily sat in the shade and revelled in the fact that we had finally made it to the Omo Valley, laughing about how our worry about the big, raging river had caused us so much grief in the last two weeks.

Coming from the glorious, empty vastness of Lake Turkana I was surprised to see tourists in such great numbers visiting Ethiopia. We shared the observation that the Ethiopia under our feet was not the Ethiopia that we had expected to see. We had been braced to see drought-stricken deserts and starving babies surrounded by masses of flies. Instead we saw lush, green valleys, mountains of respectable height, and beautiful, colourful locals with strong physiques who were proud of their tribal customs and history. I also had not expected to see the quantity of new Toyota Land Cruisers belonging to every possible non-governmental organization under the sun. Ethiopia was NGO central, and out of all the recipients of good fortune here, Toyota surely topped the list.

The next day we crossed one of the rivers that could have been our river of misinformation, but it was nowhere near where we thought it would be. Across the 15-metre riverbed, the damp sand only held a trickle of water. In the end, we barely got our tires wet.

Two days later, an overnight rainstorm filled the riverbed one metre deep. Tourists trapped on the other side had no choice but to wait it out until the water level dropped and then a road construction grader could pull their Land Cruisers through. This was indeed the river of ill repute.

Not being in any rush to get to Addis Ababa, Ethiopia's capital, we lingered in as many towns as we could before getting there, including Arba Minch, where I took a dirty hotel room in the middle of town while Guy and Marleen stayed on the outskirts in their truck. My hotel apparently came with Bart, my new English-speaking friend. Bart was a

local teenager who was always ready to show me the local restaurants and creatively ordered my meals so they would arrive on two plates. Despite the obvious gastronomic reasons for Bart's friendship with me, I was happy to have him around, as he was able to answer many of my questions about local culture and in particular about the qat tradition.

The river we had worried about.

Qat is a leaf that is chewed in large quantities for its amphetamine-like buzz and the energy and loss of hunger that come from chewing it. Unlike the coca leaves of Bolivia, which permit harder work with less fatigue, qat makes people far less productive. Any energy and euphoria derived from the leaves isn't squandered on work; instead, it is put completely into relaxing and socializing with other qat chewers. The leaves are most potent when fresh, so qat-chewing areas grind to a halt every afternoon when the newly picked leaves arrive in town.

When I told Bart I wanted to try some qat, he took me by the hand up a dusty side road to the concrete block house where his sister lived. We said hello to the girls working out front and parted the Rasta-coloured bead curtain covering the entrance to a dark sitting room. After my eyes adjusted to the low light, I could see walls lined with cushions. We sat in a corner where I could watch the door and the methods of the girls. We had joined a group of three other young men who were content to accept my hello with a lazy, wordless handshake. My foreigner status was impossible to hide and I did not bother to try.

Bart's sister, who I was beginning to gather was not really his sister, presented me with a bag of leaves at my feet, as well as a bowl of peanuts and a bowl of sugar. Her job was to keep a steady supply of leaves and accessories in front of all of the chewers. If all the men were happily chewing and chatting, she would come over and sit in front of me on her knees, choosing the best leaves to place in my mouth. Occasionally she made a large leaf into a scoop and gathered up sugar with it, pushing the whole thing into my mouth, the sugar doing wonders to balance the sharp taste of the plain leaf. A bottle of Coke was brought in – the sweetness of the drink was also used to make the leaves more palatable.

We stayed for hours, consuming endless cups of tea and a forest's worth of leaves while Britney Spears looked down on me from her poster on one wall and Ronaldo and his soccer ball looked down on me from the other. My hands shook as I talked and talked. I got back to the hotel after midnight. I remember lying on the bed shivering and wondering why I couldn't fall asleep. I eventually did and woke up tired, with a headache that could be attributed to the litres of Coke and sweet tea that I had drunk the night before, let alone the qat.

I arrived in Addis Ababa in December. I found a guesthouse that let me put my tent up in the courtyard, and got to work on finishing the details of the 2008 version of the calendar. I emailed the organizers of the Calgary and Edmonton motorcycle shows and asked permission again for my family to sell the calendars there on my behalf, which was kindly given.

2008 Calendar.

I picked up from the internet that the Iranian foreign embassies located in the countries close to Iran were not giving visas out as freely as travellers would expect. Betting that the Iranian embassy in Addis Ababa was far enough away to be isolated from these problems, I went there to apply for my Iranian visa. In addition to the normal application details such as name, address and passport number, I also had to write a paragraph on why I wanted to visit the Islamic Republic of Iran. In the waiting room where I sat were several pamphlets on the benefits of Islam and I pulled a few mighty impressive quotes out of them to bolster my argument.

When I submitted my application, I was informed that all visas must be approved by Tehran and to return in a month. That was fine by me, as it allowed me to take a tour of the northern half of Ethiopia and return for New Year's Eve in the city. I returned to the Iranian embassy on my scheduled date and was asked to fill out all of the application forms again, as they could not find my papers from before. In fifteen minutes, my visa was ready, making me suspicious about the story of Tehran needing to approve each individual application.

Shortly before I planned to leave Addis Ababa, I met Robbo and his

Faces of Ethiopia.

Honda Africa Twin. He had started in London the previous year, travelling down the west coast of Africa and then up the east coast on the long way back to Australia. We were both going east through Djibouti, Yemen and Oman and decided that it would be wise to do this part together as we would need to hire a boat to take us across the Gulf of Aden to Yemen, something neither of us had any idea how to do.

Our exit from Ethiopia was delayed a few days when Robbo came down with malaria. Treatment was a three-day course of pills, and on the third day he felt well enough to make a run for Djibouti, an all-day ride parallel to the Somalia border. Every smouldering garbage pile we passed caused Robbo to mutter, "Get me the hell out of Africa and give me the Middle East!" Little did we know that it would not be long before he was yearning for Africa again.

The former French colony of Djibouti is now a predominately Muslim country known primarily for its French and American military bases and its deep sea port (run by Dubai) that acts as the entry point of goods for both Eritrea to the north and Ethiopia to the west. With the notable exception of salt, practically all consumer goods have to be imported and taxes kick the price of everything through the roof, forcing foreigners to grit their teeth and fork over $8 if they want a bottle of Heineken beer.

Perhaps dragged down by being home to the lowest point on the African continent (nearby Lake Assal is 156 metres below sea level), Djibouti City displayed the most depressing daily life that I saw in Africa. The outskirts of the city were a collection of squatters' camps, massive dirt parking lots for waiting transport trucks, and smoking rubbish heaps.

Inside the city, men chewed qat, dragging productivity to a standstill whenever a fresh batch of leaves arrived. In the shade of trees and walls everywhere, men reclined and socialized, stopping their conversations only long enough to stuff a few more leaves into their cheeks.

Robbo's and my plan was to go directly to the Yemeni embassy and apply for our visas, then find a cheap hotel. If the best we could do was $50 a night for an awful budget hotel, we decided we would prefer to drive back into the desert and camp in the wild. We easily found the city

ABOVE: Robbo cruises past relics of the 1977 Ogaden war between Ethiopia and Somalia.

BELOW: The restless border with Somalia is just behind the mountains, but we saw little traffic in the area and the roads were in very good condition.

centre, which was strangely quiet for 3 p.m. on a Thursday. At the Yemeni embassy we met Riad, the general-purpose helper guy. He was all smiles and could jump back and forth between five languages, depending on who he was talking to.

He told us that the embassy was now closed and would be closed the

On Sunday afternoon, AbdulKarim got us through the port's security gates and we checked in with the port police on our way to the boat. I was expecting our boat to be somewhat less...wooden, but she looked sturdy and worn enough to have survived the crossing many times.

Once the ramps were laid against the hull to load the bikes, the action started up. The lingering dockworkers knew that as long as they laid a hand on the bikes coming onto the boat, they could claim payment for helping to load our cargo. Fights broke out among them as we tried to get the bikes on without anybody ending up in the water.

Once the three bikes and our luggage were on board, the leader of the dockworkers came up to me demanding payment for his guys having loading the boat. I told him plainly that our price included getting the bikes onto the boat and that he should take his complaint to AbdulKarim. Then his men started to pipe up, getting involved in the argument. I walked 500 metres with the group of workers to the office where AbdulKarim was. His eyes popped when the mass of dockworkers came into the room and began loudly voicing their complaints all at once. I yelled over the group that we had paid in full and any extra charges were the responsibility of AbdulKarim. The dockworkers started at me again, and I kept saying, "AbdulKarim...

ABOVE: Our cook and his kitchen.

AbdulKarim," as I backed out of the office, closing the door and leaving behind a beehive of squawking men.

The sun lingered long enough to give us a final African sunset, and by 7 p.m. we were underway: twenty-four people, three motorcycles, and two goats. Robbo and I had both spent about 17 months in Africa and were both anxious to get into the Middle East with its lure of Arabian legends, incense, frankincense, and ancient Muslim culture. The full moon was coming up and I asked the cook on board when we would be arriving in Yemen.

"Tomorrow," he replied, "Insha'Allah."

Mursi woman from the Omo Valley in Ethiopia with her distinctive lower lip clay disk.

CHAPTER 6
MIDDLE EAST

Upon closer inspection, the boat taking us from Africa to Yemen was soundly built and its design moved us determinedly through the water. The back quarter of the deck had a cover under which most of the passengers lay and chatted; the below-deck area held the cargo and the chugging diesel engine. The captain sat on the roof at the very back, steering the boat with a dangling foot and rarely moving from his perch.

The toilet deserves a special mention. It was a small wooden box hanging off the side of the boat. It required a backwards half-squat to get into and nervous users had to be mindful of keeping their feet on the two narrow planks that made up the limited floor. One hand braced against the door to keep it from coming open when the boat pitched to the right; the other was used to remain upright when the boat pitched to the left. Twenty feet below the user, the ocean slipped by, along with whatever happened to fall out of the bottom of the box.

Robbo and Michael tried to sleep beside the motorcycles while I hung my hammock at mid-ship. As I drifted off to sleep, I watched large supertankers pass us in the moonlight at three times our speed, leaving barely a ripple. The moon was now high and this crossing of the Gulf of Aden certainly qualified as one of my full-moon celebrations.

In early morning, the cook brought us breakfast of dhal, baguettes, and sweet black tea. We were still a kilometre offshore, but we had our first glimpses of long beaches and the mud brick houses of the Arabian Peninsula. No trees could be seen and the whole place looked barren, dusty, and hot. I wondered how many ships like ours had made this journey over the last 3000 years with their holds full of spices, frankincense, slaves or salt.

At midday the port appeared and we pulled up to the concrete dock after being on the water for 18 hours. Already moored were a huge red oil tanker and a smaller livestock ship. It was first-come, first-served at these docks, so these earlier arrivals had secured the best spots, leaving us to wedge ourselves under the ropes that held the other ships still. We got as close as we could, but our mooring still left us a metre from the dock.

Although AbdulKarim had assured us that off-loading the bikes was also covered in our $130 fee, none of us had believed him. Sure enough, another $50 was demanded from the dockworkers, so we opted to do it ourselves. After all, how hard could it be?

We found two wide planks and fixed them so they stretched from the edge of the boat onto the dock across the metre of water. Robbo and Michael lifted the front wheel of the first bike off the deck and hoisted it up onto the ramp, which

ABOVE: Trying to catch some sleep during the ride over.

BELOW: Our disembarkation was more pleasant than it was for the camels being off-loaded next to us, who were unloaded by a crane with a sling around their bellies.

was about a metre above the deck, while I steadied the bike in this wheelie position from the rear. Robbo then jumped onto the ramp and held the front wheel steady for Michael and me to lift the rest of the bike onto the ramp.

The bike's weight was now completely supported on this two-foot-wide plank over the sea. Robbo steered with one hand, held the front brake with the other, and walked slowly backwards down to the dock while Michael and I held our breath. If the bike slipped off the ramp, there would be no way to recover it. We managed to offload all three bikes without issue, much to the disappointment of the dockworkers who had gathered in the shade to watch us.

Geographically, Yemen is only 20 kilometres away from Africa, but the cultural differences between the two are colossal. We had stepped off the boat onto a land where the separation of church and state and the democratic rules of life that we grew up with were no longer valid and held no authority. The rules here were put into place 1300 years ago by the Prophet Muhammad, and still laid claim to all aspects of Islamic public and private life.

The killings of the previous week did not help with my feelings of uneasiness while riding. Robbo bravely led out the initial leg while I looked suspiciously behind every crumbled building and abandoned car, planning my escape if we were attacked. With every change of terrain I re-formulated my get-away plans and wondered if we had really made the smartest decision in going there.

Near sunset we got close to the city of Taizz, marvelling at how a city of 330,000 people could be so quiet. Robbo filled in the gap for me.

"Where are all the women?" he asked.

I had not noticed, but he was right. In effect, we only saw half the population of the city. And when we did see a woman, we never really saw her – just a figure cloaked from head to toe in black, with nothing but her eyes showing. In Yemen, immigrant men from India, Pakistan, or Bangladesh fill most of the public jobs traditionally held by women, such as tailors, cooks, and cleaners.

A police car stopped us as we entered Taizz. I gave him a piece of paper with my name, passport number, and a brief description of my trip written on it that Riad had translated into Arabic for me before we left Djibouti. The policeman was glad to escort us, with his siren wailing and lights blazing, to a hotel for tourists. As we unloaded the motor-cycles, the Minister of Tourism for the area arrived and he invited us to stay at a fancier hotel downtown, courtesy of the city government. We declined his offer, but did agree to meet an English-speaking guide the next day for a tour of the city and to meet other government officials for an apparent photo opportunity. Tourism brought much-needed income to Yemen, as their reserves of oil and gas were not as plentiful as those in the neighbouring countries of Saudi Arabia and Oman. Understandably, many tourists had cancelled their visits due to the recent killings. Perhaps the Minister thought that a picture in the newspaper of three handsome, rugged adventurers would convince them all to reconsider.

Two days in the historic capital city of Sana'a fostered a healthy respect for the engineers and builders who worked with mud, cob, and sparse

ABOVE AND RIGHT: Getting the Canadian's opinion on the tourist killings in Yemen.

amounts of wood to create tall, multi-storey buildings and tall, multi-family houses that date back hundreds of years. I forgave the original city planners for the congestion, the random layout of roads, and the twisty perplexity of the many skinny alleys that created massive confusion for newcomers. I suspect the planners didn't anticipate their work having such longevity when Sana'a was founded 2500 years ago.

The nighttime market was held in the old walled fort that had been swallowed up whole by the growing city around it. Salt, spices, frankincense, fruit, bread and silverware were sold as they have been for thousands of years. New to the market were the stalls with sunglasses, plumbing supplies and cheap flip-flops. I passed a door with a handwritten 'internet' sign in English above it, and used an ancient computer to check in with Colette.

In Africa it was more convenient to keep in touch by text messages on the cell phone, as SIM cards were available in most countries for a dollar or less. Cell phones were popular in Yemen, but buying a SIM card was a mission, so Colette and I resigned ourselves to relying on the internet for communication until I reached North America.

My initial discovery of internet cafés in remote parts of the world bothered me, as I had tried hard to get myself into places far away and far different from Canada. I selfishly wanted these areas to remain remote and untouched by the trappings of the modern world that I had left behind. By the time I reached Yemen, however, I was able to see the internet for what it was providing these areas – a technology that allowed those who were online to socialize, be entertained, and most importantly get access to information about local and international events.

Out of all the countries that I had been to, only the Muslim governments had felt threatened enough by the internet to censure it and block specified content. The clergy and the bureaucrats have not recognized that the world of the web is the playing field of the students, and the old solutions of state media control and choking off incoming news by the traditional means of simply ignoring it have little effect on the craftiness of the web-folks. It only works on rural townsfolk and those who cannot afford the luxury of a computer or trips to the internet café. For these people, the regular government-approved media and gossip – always a powerful medium – are the only sources of information. This is setting up a divide between the poorer, less educated, state-informed population and the schooled youths and adults who are connected to the outside world via the internet and its myriad of opinions, views and arguments.

Yemen has only had access to secular education since the mid 1960s, but the kids are learning quickly. The high school and college students who cram the popular internet cafés have no problems ducking around the obstacles set up by the government to get access to any content they wish to see, leaving me to suspect that any real societal progress for Yemen will come through the ADSL line.

The road from Sana'a to the south coast would have been more interesting if we could have shaken the baby blue Hyundai Santa Fe that kept following us. Unfortunately, the car belonged to our personal police escort, who had been assigned to us in Sana'a. Our resigned attitudes took an adjustment when we crested the Nagil Thirah Pass that had us laugh-

ing with amazement. The road snuck down the steep mountainside in countless tight hairpin turns and across the crests of buttresses. There were more mountains and more hairpins as far as we could see to the desert floor in the dusty distance. It was a well-constructed and scenic road, and if we had been alone we would have gone up and down it a few times to enjoy it properly.

Our little caravan started down the mountainside in second gear, but came to a halt behind a collection of cars that had stopped at an accident scene. A small pickup truck had obviously missed one of the upper turns and tumbled to land upside-down onto the road below.

As our escort radioed in the accident, we snuck by, driving over parts of the broken engine twenty feet from the truck. We stopped to see the driver, but there was not much to look at. Two purple hands stuck out between the truck and the pavement, the rest was a guess. Fluids from the truck and the driver splashed halfway up the door and left a widening pool that crept down the road. Predestined fate is one of the pillars of the Islam faith, and it was obviously the prevailing opinion that it was this guy's turn to go. As a result the others were not affected very much about the whole affair. None of the onlookers seemed sad or hysterical, and eventually our escorts nonchalantly gave us an "Okay, time to go," as if we had just stopped to smell the flowers.

ABOVE: Our guard checks out the view from the top of the pass, his cheek bulging from a mouthful of qat.

LEFT: Michael and Robbo negotiate the tight maze of alleys in Sana'a. The city's architecture and old fort have garnered it a World Heritage City designation from the United Nations.

By late afternoon, we had been through a dozen checkpoints, and the constant confusion that we created at each one was tiring. Our travelling permission papers were collected, our passports looked at, and phone calls made to find out from somebody what to do with us, or who had to drive us to the next station. We had hoped to reach the coast before nightfall, but at our last checkpoint for the day, the sun had already slipped behind the mountains and we still had 40 kilometres to go. Driving at night – escort or no escort – is never wise, so we demanded that the guards either let us go ahead or get somebody into one of the bloody cars and take us to the coast before it was pitch dark.

I pulled out the newspaper article of us from the interview with the Minister of Tourism in Taizz, and made as if we were important travellers to hurry them along. The article was in Arabic and I had no idea what it said, but apparently the text was not as important as I had hoped, because the guards handed me back the article and told us to wait some more.

Twenty minutes later, when the sun had fully set, we left our last checkpoint, with Yemen's only slow driver behind the wheel of our police escort. If the intention was to transport us safely from one check stop to the next, it made no sense to have a police car with lights flashing driving slowly in front of us. Any terrorist could see us miles away and not even have to hide as they shot at us from the side of the road, slipping back into the night.

We arrived at the coast at night and in a grumpy mood. At the last police checkpoint outside the coastal town of Shaqra, we were informed that we were not allowed to go into the city as there were "bad men with guns," and that we were not allowed to camp in the wild. There was little option but to make camp behind their compound. We chose the spot that smelled the least like piss but still kept us out of the wind. We were thankful that at least we were setting up the camp in the dark and couldn't see how bad our surroundings were until the next morning.

With the smell of everyone's morning ablutions wafting through my tent, I woke up to a foul start. Michael was busy pulling a never-ending stream of interesting things from his massive custom-built panniers. A

The most unpleasant campsite in Yemen.

large tarp was put on the dirt, followed by a small collapsible table and two folding chairs – surprising, as he travelled alone. Robbo had the kettle on, and Michael brought out his breakfast kit of thin sachets of instant cappuccinos.

"That's stupid," I thought. "Does he think we're camping at the Hilton?"

I pulled out my plastic Coke bottle of instant coffee crystals and made a cup of coffee, squirting a bit of Nestlé sweetened condensed milk into it for flavour. It was revolting, but comforting in a manly way.

On this coastal road we hoped to catch a glimpse of our bicycle friend Lars. I had met Lars at Victoria Falls in Zambia the year before and Robbo had crossed paths with him in Africa as well. Lars had cycled from Sweden to Cape Town, then to South America, before coming to the Middle East. For a few months we had been sending emails back and forth to each other, trying to manage to meet up again, but our paths hadn't yet crossed.

By 9 a.m., our escort had caught another group of police vehicles, and in the midst of them was Lars with his bicycle. He was having a miserable time. His options were to have a police escort drive slowly behind him as he cycled, or to sit in the back of the escort truck while they ferried him from check stop to check stop. Two nights before he had waited at a check stop for two hours before he convinced them to let him go. He had to promise to go directly to the next town and check in with the police. Once out of range of the escorts, he jumped into the bush to make camp for the night. At nightfall the police looked for him and were not impressed when they found him cooking rice behind a tree. They put him

Our escort was not usually this obvious, but it was nice to have them on our side.

in the truck and brought him to the next town, where they watched as he paid for a hotel room and then accompanied him up to it.

We spent two more days with our escorts before they allowed us to make our way alone to the border on the final two days of our journey

Robbo and Lars in Yemen.

through the country. It was difficult to be angry with them for making sure we were safe, but their presence sterilized the trip. Their security efforts were good for tourism, but bad for tourists. Of course, my feelings might have been coloured by the fact that we were now close to the end of Yemen and our safety had never been jeopardized.

Lars wanted to get into Oman quickly so he could start to ride his bicycle again. We offered to give him a lift to the border, and divided his gear, including his bike, among the three motorcycles to get there.

ABOVE: All of Lars' belongings distributed onto our bikes. Note the bad placement of the yellow dry bag relative to my motorcycle's exhaust pipe.

BELOW: Lesson learned.

We were all anxious to get out of Yemen. The constant police escorts, the litter, pollution, and inability to explore freely were wearing thin. Robbo was already reminiscing about Africa and Michael and I passed the evenings by planning our Oman routes. Having only managed to pedal 20 kilometres in Yemen, Lars was the most anxious of all of us to get to Oman and travel again under his own power.

We planned a noodles and tuna feast to celebrate getting through Yemen alive, and looked for a bush camp close to Oman so we could do

the border formalities first thing in the morning. A rocky trail led down to a clearing where we wanted to set up camp. Near the bottom of the trail, Michael misjudged the width of Lars' bicycle, which was strapped to the back of his motorcycle. He slammed the bicycle's rear wheel into a jutting rock, destroying it. Lars' bad luck in Yemen was continuing right

to the bitter end. He would now have to join us as we made our way into Oman.

Our first views of Oman were impressive, even before we officially entered the country. The border officials were polite and in uniform, and computers sped our entry formalities along. The presence of public garbage cans struck me as odd, but would help explain the notable lack of litter. Qat is illegal in Oman and the ubiquitous small plastic bags that it comes in are absent as well.

On our first night, we shared a hotel room that allowed us to get laundry done and catch up on internet work. Robbo and Michael left the next day for the capital city of Muscat, as Michael had to catch a flight to Germany and Robbo had McVisions of his first McDonald's since South Africa.

Lars and I tried unsuccessfully to find a rear wheel to fit his bicycle. Oman was not yet set up for budget tourists and our hotel

LEFT, TOP: Robbo and Lars discuss plans for the next day's ride.

LEFT, CENTRE: Another lesson learned.

LEFT, BOTTOM: Our last wild camp in Yemen, finally on our own.

room was too expensive to stay longer and leisurely explore other options, so Lars hopped on the bus for a twelve-hour ride to Muscat to continue his search for a wheel.

In a later email, he informed me that Muscat came up empty so he journeyed another five hours on the bus to U.A.E. and the modern city of Dubai. There, Lars found the wheel, but he had lost his spirit for the Arabic Peninsula. He boarded a plane to Eastern Europe and rode home to Sweden.

I started my four-day drive to

ABOVE: I wait out the hot sun while Michael fixes a flat tire.

BELOW: The long, hot road to Muscat.

Scene from a small desert town.

slight gorge or behind a hill. The nomadic Bedouin people of old Oman still have the love of the desert in their blood, although many have traded in their camels for Land Cruisers. Their history of desert dwelling means a level of respect is given to anybody who chooses to sleep in the wild, and my nights camping there were free of any worry about malicious nighttime visitors.

The city of Muscat did a wonderful job of presenting its impressive history and culture to the important tourist market. Teams of cleaners from India, Pakistan and Bangladesh worked at all hours to keep the walkways and streets spotless (in fact, I learned it was possible to receive a fine for driving a dirty car). A tolerant attitude towards western business allowed Starbucks and McDonald's to open shop beside traditional markets full of perfumes, frankincense, silks, gold, silver and woodworkers.

Five hours west in the city of Dubai, U.A.E., the progress is more aggressive but not nearly as aesthetically pleasing. Dubai is reinvesting its oil money into tourism and infrastructure projects, but at the same time, is not immune to tripping over itself

Bedouin woman at the fish market.

Muscat by choosing the coastal road instead of the inland, 1000-kilometre asphalt highway. Deserts and oil fields dominated the southern half of Oman and there were unlimited options for camping in the wild. Finding a spot was as easy as driving a few kilometres on any dirt road into a

as it tries to become the world's biggest or best in as many categories as it can afford to.

ABOVE: A quick weekend ride ends with a front flat tire on the freeway and some road rash from the subsequent crash.

BELOW: Massive building projects made the roads thick with construction traffic.

My Dubai contacts that I had received in South Africa turned out to be more helpful than I could have ever hoped for. Johan and Charmaine had ridden their BMW from South Africa to Dubai three years ago. They had stopped to work and raise funds for the rest of their travels, and were now gearing up to leave again. They offered me a spare room while I sorted out my Central Asian visa applications – and another visa for Iran. The Iranian visa that I had picked up in Ethiopia had expired before I had a chance to enter. I applied again at the busy Iranian consulate in Dubai and was told to come back in two weeks to pick it up.

After two weeks I began calling every day to give my name and application number, only to be told to "try again this afternoon or maybe tomorrow, Insha'Allah." The embassy refused to give any more details on why there was a delay. I waited another two weeks, during which Johan and Charmaine received their Iranian visa with only a one-day wait. (With a bit of internet digging, I think I found part of the answer. Five months earlier, in December of 2007, the Canadian ambassador had been expelled from Iran in a diplomatic pissing match. In January, additional trade sanctions against Iran had been enforced by the USA, Canada, and England. This may explain why they had issued me a visa earlier but were ignoring me now).

While I waited impatiently for my visa, I considered other options. Iran is a ferry ride north of Dubai. Assuming my visa came through, I would have a fairly straightforward passage through Iran and northeast to the glorious high-altitude Pamir Highway in Tajikistan, then to Russia, then Mongolia, and back to Russia. Then I would fly over the Bering Sea to Alaska and drive home.

Without the visa for Iran, my routing options would become more complicated. I would need to find another way to get to Tajikistan. Flying the motorcycle over inconvenient countries by air cargo was always an option, but it defeated the spirit of riding around the world. I had skipped Colombia when flying from Panama to Ecuador and regretted it.

With the maps of Central Asia on the floor, I looked at other route choices. Across the Persian Gulf to the west of Iran was Iraq, off-limits due to the ongoing conflict there. To the east of Iran was Pakistan. There was no ferry service to Pakistan, but I could get a cargo ship to bring the bike over. Leaving to Pakistan would solve the immediate issue of how to leave Dubai, but toss me headlong into another.

Besides Iran, there are three ways to leave Pakistan. To the east is India, but it was a driving dead-end for me because if I kept going east after India, I would eventually run into Myanmar, which I would not be allowed to enter. To the north of Pakistan is China, which charges $1100 for a five-day escort to the nearby country of Kazakhstan. Even if I wanted to pursue this option, there was a two-month wait for a guide to prepare the paperwork for the vehicle, so that was out.

West of Pakistan is another rugged country that allows swift access to the bottom of the Pamir Highway and allows travellers to reach Tajikistan, Kyrgyzstan and Kazakhstan. The only problem is that this country – Afghanistan – was having issues of its own and my contact from within Afghanistan told me to drive through it would be "absolutely a bad idea in the current security environment." So now what?

My visa for U.A.E. expired soon and without the Iranian visa, my only choice was to send the bike to Karachi, Pakistan by ocean freight and then drive it to the capital of Islamabad. To get to Tajikistan from there, I would need to rely on local rogue airlines – long banned in EU airspace – that operated flights between Central Asian cities. A quick stop to the airport in Islamabad could tell me if one of the crumbling planes were going anywhere close to the Pamir Highway.

I crated the bike at BMW Dubai. The truck that delivered the packed crate to the port went past Johan's place and the driver was kind enough to drop me off at an internet café near the house.

I just about shit myself reading my latest email. My Iranian visa was approved and I could enter at any time.

I called the shipping office to cancel the shipment, but they were closed. When I checked in the next morning, I was informed that it was too late to stop the ocean shipment to Pakistan, but that did not overly bother me. I was content with the fact that I did not need to fly over Afghanistan on a dodgy plane from Pakistan to Tajikistan. I just had to detour 5500 kilometres around it.

With my Iranian visa confirmed, I could now plan the road route to the Pamir Highway. North of Iran are the former Soviet republics of Turkmenistan, Uzbekistan, Tajikistan, Kyrgyzstan, and Kazakhstan. Visas are required for all of these countries, so I spent my last days in Dubai visiting the various embassies and trying to sort them out. Visa applications for multiple countries were tricky. On each application you listed the entry and exit dates, which usually allowed a 30-day stay. The difficult part was choosing the right amount of overlap between one country and the next. It was possible that you could arrive at a country before your visa started and would not be permitted to enter. Or your visa to the next country could expire before you got there (like the case with my first visa for Iran), forcing you to find an embassy to start the application process all over again. I was fortunate that Dubai was home to many different foreign embassies, and I was happy to receive a three-day transit visa for

Turkmenistan, thirty days for Kyrgyzstan, and thirty days for Kazakhstan. Uzbekistan and Tajikistan would be done closer to those countries.

A colourful bus in Karachi.

Dubai was also the last modern city that I planned to see until Anchorage and I took advantage of it by stocking up on oil filters from the BMW dealer and upgrading my camera again, this time to a Nikon D80. The day before I flew to Pakistan, I also loaded up with a box of terribly convenient 3-in-1 coffee sachets – the kind I had secretly scorned Michael the German for using – that included a bit of instant coffee, a bit of sugar, and a bit of powered creamer in a plastic tube for individual use. Michael would have been proud.

Rob at CMG Online had given me a contact in Karachi, and I was quick to email him in search of a floor to crash on. Richard was happy to oblige, but at the last minute was called out of town. His roommate, Taimur, kindly offered to take over as my host and be my local guide while I waited for the motorcycle to clear Pakistani customs.

Taimur showed me a fascinating side of Pakistani culture that I would never have seen in my normal travels. We bought beer and whisky wrapped in conspicuous-looking brown paper bags from unmarked shops, went to late night parties with actors and models, and made trips to small private beaches. Taimur refused to let me pay for anything and every night he had the best Pakistani curries, kebabs and fresh tandoori breads brought in from local vendors.

I had hoped in my western way that a day or two would be plenty for the paperwork necessary for my bike to clear customs at the Port of Karachi, but it became apparent that I wouldn't actually collect the BMW until a week longer than I'd hoped.

Eventually I was allowed access to the customs depot and assembled the bike. The battery was dead, but a push start down the loading ramp got me running. As I left the customs area, the last step in the process was showing the guard at the exit gate all of my stamped paperwork. He was from Afghanistan and his light green eyes played off his ill-fitting woolen grey waistcoat. His pistol's holster hung lazily from his shoulder and he smiled as I approached him.

"America?" he inquired.

"No, Canada," I replied, handing him my papers for his approval.

"Want hash?" he asked.

"Hey, no thanks."

As anxious as I was to leave Karachi, there was one important stop I wanted to make. The buses and trucks had a special form of decoration that I had fallen in love with, and I wanted desperately to find someone to decorate my bike in this style as well. Adhesive coloured reflective sheeting was cut into patterns, symbols, names or designs and carefully added in layers to every possible outside surface of the big vehicles. If Pakistan could be governed with the same love and attention to detail as its truck decorators display, the country would be a world leader. Taimur found a local shop where four men got to work on my bike. Four hours and ten dollars later I drove away on my artwork.

My newly decorated BMW and I were ready to blast through the rest of Pakistan to Iran, pick up the Uzbekistan visa and get back on my original time schedule. It was 3001 kilometres to Tehran and I had 12 days to get there. Two long days of travel through Pakistan would get me to the Iranian border, leaving ten days to get to Tehran.

As dusk fell, I arrived in Quetta, my first overnight stop. Bordering

The highway through the Baluchistan Desert.

THE UNIVERSITY OF GRAVEL ROADS

Afghanistan, this city has always had markets filled with locally grown fruit, camels, Afghan refugees, and traders doing a brisk business across the borders. These days Quetta has another important role. Supplies and equipment bound for NATO forces in Afghanistan that are sent by sea arrive at the port of Karachi and enter Afghanistan through Quetta. The trucks that carry the goods between the port and Quetta have access to secure, guarded compounds along the road that allow for safe overnight stays or daytime rest stops. While wandering the port of Karachi, I had met the man responsible for the logistics of these shipments. He gave me his business card and told me to call if I needed help along the road or a safe place to stay for the night, but in the end, I made it safely after only 11 hours of riding.

The next day's ride from Quetta to Iran through the Baluchistan Desert made me more than a little nervous. The regions of Baluchistan and neighbouring southern Afghanistan often made the news with reports of tribal violence, and there had been recent tourist kidnappings along this route. The terrain doesn't reassure, either, with wide-open, dusty plains that fold into sterile, far-off hills on either side of the road.

I left Quetta early after filling up with fuel. On the outskirts of the city I waited until I could fall in with a convoy of local Land Cruisers who were also heading west, figuring there would be safety in numbers.

The road was asphalt and better than I expected and our little convoy made good time until we reached the first police checkpoint. The local Land Cruisers were waved through, but I was stopped and told to go into a little mud hut police office and leave the usual details about my passport and motorcycle.

There were ultimately a dozen or so of these checkpoints along the way, but since I was riding solo I was glad to see them. It broke up the journey and allowed me to relax a little more with each stop. The police were good-natured, and tea always appeared when I removed my helmet, but the soaring temperatures made me decline. The good asphalt road that I started on eventually turned into a one-lane bad asphalt road, and the occasional oncoming large truck made no contest about who was going to remain there and

Topping up with fuel from the side of the road. Note the crash in the background - not an uncommon sight.

who would drive off into the desert to avoid being hit.

After a twelve-hour day, I pulled into the dusty town of Taftan as the sun started its drop across the horizon. Taftan is the border town between Pakistan and Iran, and I took a room at a run-down hotel to watch the evening action unfold from the second-floor balcony. Moneychangers squatted in the sand with wads of bills in canvas bags at their feet, waiting for business. Men driving baby-blue pickup trucks filled plastic barrels with fuel and drove back into the Baluchistan Desert, from where they would cross illegally into Afghanistan and sell it on the black market.

Although I had arrived with no real trouble, the worry and heat of the day's ride had exhausted me. I was also stressed about the following day's border formalities. I did not expect getting out of Pakistan to present a problem. It was the Iranian border complex around the corner that had me worried, specifically for the motorcycle. When I had applied for the carnet to start the second leg of the trip, the deposit for Iran had been raised from 120% to 250% of the value of the vehicle, which for me meant an additional $6250. I did not have that much extra money, so I had simply left Iran off the list of permissible countries.

So now my personal visa was in order, but on the back of my carnet, it explicitly stated that my bike was not covered to enter Iran. No carnet? No entry. If I was turned away at the border, I would need to drive back through the desert to Islamabad and try the airplane cargo method.

I figured what the customs officials did not see wouldn't hurt them, so I placed a small drop of crazy glue on the carnet's back cover and opened the front, gluing them together. This left the book exposed to the pages that the customs guys needed to fill out, and obscured the pages that – in my opinion – they did not need to see.

Having solved this little problem to the best of my abilities, I retired early, but later woke in a pool of sweat. The wobbly ceiling fan pushed all the stifling heat from the room onto me, and at 5 a.m., I gave up trying to sleep. I took refuge on the second floor balcony and watched the locals wake up on the rooftops of all the buildings, fold up their mattresses, and disappear inside – a much wiser choice for a sleeping arrangement.

I arrived at the Taftan customs office early, and twenty minutes and a cup of tea later I finished the Pakistan exit formalities and drove the hundred metres to the Iranian border post. Inside the gate, two policemen checked my documents and recorded my details in a thick paper ledger. I kept the conversation light to distract them from my little glue trick and to hide my nerves. They showed me the way to the main customs office, where the computers, air conditioning, and spotless tile floor were in glaring contrast to the old, stuffy, wooden office with its massive paper notebooks back on the Pakistani side. Given the choice, I would have preferred to bluff my way into a country without computers and without security cameras watching me from every angle.

My passport and carnet disappeared into a large office with glass walls, landing on the head guy's desk. He scrutinized my documentation, flipping through previous entries and noting the customs stamps from Yemen, Oman, U.A.E., and Africa. He stopped to answer his mobile phone and while laughing and talking he opened the cover pages, not enough to rip the glue spot, but enough to be able to see Islamic Republic of Iran crossed off in big black marker.

I was cooked.

I couldn't believe I had tried to get away with such a stupid stunt. Now, because I would have to travel back, I had lost even more time. My trip to the Pamir Highway would now be out of reach. I had spent hundreds of dollars on visas to countries that I wouldn't use, and I wasn't even sure Pakistan would let me back in, as my visa had been cancelled when I left.

The customs official threw the carnet onto the neighbouring desk and continued chatting on the phone. I watched with disbelief as my carnet went down the chain of desks – stamp, stamp, stamp! Either he did not care or it did not register with him that I was illegally importing a motorcycle into Iran.

I was too nervous to smile broadly, but I had a storm of joy brewing in my belly. When they insisted that I travel with a policeman for the next 100 kilometres, I was only too happy to rearrange the luggage to accom-

OPPOSITE: Wind towers are Persian buildings that use natural ventilation to cool interior living spaces. The photo captures the second level of the Aga Zadeh House flanked by the full moon, and the Friday Mosque of Yazd in the background.

modate him on the back. I was less happy with the policeman when I later realized that at some point in the journey he had hung my dry bag over the left-hand side of the bike where the hot exhaust gases melted another hole through the bag, right next to the Yemen-burned hole that I had just patched. At the next city, my passenger escort was traded in for motorized ones, and an assortment of small motorcycles and police cars

The Bridge of the 33 Arches, its teahouse, and the Zayandeh River in Esfahan.

passed me off from one to the other in the most disorganized fashion imaginable until we arrived after midnight in the ancient city of Bam and I collapsed into bed after another 12-hour day through the desert.

The next morning, I learned that a Japanese tourist had been kidnapped here seven months earlier and was still being held. I found a new appreciation for the efforts that had gone into my escorts, however bumbling they were.

I had seven days to get to Tehran, pay extra money for the quick processing of my Uzbekistan visa, exit Iran, and get through Turkmenistan before my visa for Turkmenistan ran out. I was playing a dangerously expensive game of visa roulette, where a missed visa required a re-application and the re-applying process took so long that the following visas expired like falling dominos.

From Bam, I rejoiced in my ability to ride on my own again and put in another all-day effort, this time arriving after dark in Yazd, which my guidebook claimed to be the oldest continuously inhabited city in the world – more than 3000 years. In the course of those 3000 years, nobody had bothered to build a cheap hotel with parking for motorcycles. I hired a few kids on bicycles to lead me to a tourist hotel, and they paraded me through streets of adobe buildings to a very nice spot in the old quarter that featured luxuries like air conditioning and a toilet seat. At $30 a night it blew the budget, but after seeing the well-appointed rooms I convinced myself that I needed these comforts if I was going to maintain my

This is the best exhibit in the Military Museum in Tehran. I had so many questions about this one I didn't know where to begin. Did the camel get a helmet? Earplugs? Did the guy ride it and shoot at the same time? Was there a more versatile one-hump version?

hectic pace. At the hotel I met Hussain, a retired aircraft mechanic from Tehran who now worked as a driver for a private tour guide. His English was basic, but his son and daughter spoke it well and he called them on his cell phone and asked them to translate our conversation. He invited me for tea when I reached Tehran, and his son Ali offered to help find directions and hours of operation for the embassies.

Another long day brought me to Esfahan, one of Iran's most beautiful cities. A wide, winding river split the city into north and south sides and provided a leafy green space along either bank. Locals flocked to the numerous teahouses and walking paths there while I enjoyed simply sitting on the grass to people-watch and let my eyes soak in colours other than the brown of the desert.

Since the Islamic Revolution of 1979, clerics have run Iran according to Islamic law that dictates – among many other things – appropriate clothing. Women, including female tourists, are not permitted to have an uncovered head and headscarves are mandatory. Progressive female students literally push the limits of the headscarf by showing more and more of the front half of their heads. If a religious police official walked over and pointed to an offending head, I didn't need a translator to understand that the woman was being told to return her scarf to a more "proper" position.

Conversations with Iranian men about this tradition usually suggested that the women enjoyed wearing the headscarf or even the more concealing veil, but I found it curious that none of my Iranian female friends wore it in their internet Facebook profile photo or used their real last names there either.

With my mind focused on routing rather than religious clothing laws, I accepted the fact that it would be nearly impossible to keep to my ambitious schedule. Twelve-hour days and a bad diet were taking their toll; over-optimism can be a terrible handicap when travelling.

I sat under a tree by the river with my maps and wrote up a new plan.

RIGHT: Preparations for dinner on the balcony of a small guesthouse in eastern Iran.

Allowing myself more time through Iran meant I would miss my visa times to Turkmenistan and Kyrgyzstan. I decided to re-apply for the Turkmenistan visa in Tehran and hope that it would be issued quickly. I would re-apply for the Kyrgyzstan visa in Uzbekistan.

On my second day in Tehran I called Hussain. He picked me up from my hotel and took me on a city tour that included the museums and most interesting neighbourhoods of Tehran. The following weekend, I was invited by his family to join them as they took a short vacation to a nearby town to watch the distillation of rose petals in the making of rose oil, which is often used in cosmetics and Persian food.

Each evening we returned to the house of an in-law and relaxed. In Iranian culture, there is a large emphasis on family gatherings, and members of Hussain's extended family appeared each evening to sit outside on antique carpets, drink tea, talk, and eat a small portion of the massive amounts of food that kept coming from the kitchen.

During the meals, the conversation was kept in basic English for my benefit. Other than the basic organizational details of my trip, the main topics were politics and religion, two slippery themes made more difficult with the language differences. My host family was very informed about the details of the progress in the US election and we all agreed that Obama was the only choice America had for progress. When asked what religions there are in Canada, I replied, "The big difference between Iran and Canada is that Canada has no state religion. There are many different religions to choose from if you want."

"And what are you?" they inquired.

"I don't believe in any gods," I replied, triggering quizzical looks from the other dinner guests.

"Then what do you believe in?" Before I had a chance to answer, the follow-up question came.

"And then why are we here?" And on its heels: "And how did we ever get here?"

I answered that I believed in science and reason and that we are here because of evolution.

"Oh, yes! You are from a monkey!" laughed the group.

I laughed with them. "No, not exactly, but you are thinking of the right general concept."

Tight-lipped smiles and a polite but non-committal "That's interesting..." ended that part of the conversation. I could not think of simple, non-science English words to explain the concept of evolution through the process of natural selection, so I smiled and waited for any questions to come up. None came, and after a pause the conversation started up again with a new topic.

Back in Tehran, Ali found the addresses for the embassies and emailed me directions in Persian that I printed out and gave to my taxi driver.

In a week I had the visas for the next two countries, Turkmenistan and Uzbekistan.

Many of the everyday people I talked to – the bread man or the parking attendant guy – were curious about the Western impression of Iranians. On my last day in Tehran, the lady in the post office wanted to know if westerners thought that all Iranians were terrorists. I slyly suggested that she tell me how much she was going to charge me to send a box of curios home before I answered her.

Artists showing the flags of Pakistan, Canada, and the freedom tower of Lahore.

CHAPTER 7
CENTRAL ASIA

Fuel in Iran was 40 cents per litre (the locals paid ten cents per litre) and I topped up my three tanks before getting to the border crossing with Turkmenistan. My load was made even heavier with the kilograms of dried fruit and dates that were gifts from Hussain's family. After exiting the squeaky-clean, air-conditioned offices of the Iranian immigration building, I made my way down a dusty road to the Turkmenistan border offices. At a counter stained with the greasy handprints of the masses that entered before me, a seated man took my passport and checked the details. I was instructed to turn around and pay the $13 country entry fee to a man behind me. I turned back around and handed the receipt to a man standing to the left of the seated man. He wrote down the receipt number and gave it back to the seated man, who also recorded it and stamped my passport. It was fascinating to watch how inefficient their routine was. I was finished in an hour and then began the whole ridiculous process again in another building in order to bring the motorcycle into the country. The customs offices and the people they employed were byproducts of the communist era, where everybody deserved a job, regardless of how this dragged down the efficiency of the entire process.

With the border behind me, I rode north towards the city and back in time. I spotted women in colourful long dresses bent over from the waist in the cotton and vegetable fields, their bags and overcoats slung on fence posts near the road. Wooden carts pulled by donkeys added to my feeling of leaving the modern world far behind.

I arrived at a small city at midday and took a room in the large, square, central hotel where the rooms cost $7.50, unless you were a foreigner, in which case you paid $15. Walking to the bar – which was an event to be celebrated in its own right – I was startled to see bare-headed girls wearing skirts that showed their knees. The Soviet communists had banned religious beliefs during their 66-year reign over Turkmenistan, and even with the Islamic financial support that came after independence, the country remained Muslim Lite. Religion settled in where it could alongside the entrenched artifacts of Russian culture, which included alcohol and miniskirts.

I crossed into Uzbekistan comfortable in the knowledge that there was a motorcycle-friendly hotel in the next city of Bukhara. The summer sun lingered above the cotton and corn fields, and the wind was warm. The pleasant weather helped keep people outside; the women talked on the roads and the men enjoyed tea at roadside food stalls. I knew that I could be at the hotel in an hour, have a beer and enjoy the city, and part of me wanted to do just that. But here, in the countryside, was where friendly rural folks were, and I chastised myself for wanting to be "safe" in a hotel.

ABOVE: Girls in traditional Turkmen clothes.

BELOW: A farming couple comes into town to sell produce at the market.

I circled back after seeing a group of men drinking tea at a tea shop with outdoor tables set under leafy trees. I parked, walked over, and introduced myself. They invited me to join them at their table. The elevated tables were designed so that you sat shoeless on the surface, cross-legged. The eating and serving surface was a short removable box that was placed between the guests in the middle of the table. In our case, this surface was filled with tea, then smoked trout, and then vodka.

With the help of a limited phrase book, we had a brief conversation about where I was from and what I was doing. My hosts explained that they had a small family-run restaurant and butchery. The nervous-looking cow in the back field was going to be on the menu tomorrow.

I used the international symbol for sleeping – two hands pressed together beside a tilted head – to ask if I could sleep there for the evening and more vodka came out as a reply. We drank it neat in shot glasses, with shallow bowls of pickled carrots, radishes, and cucumbers as snacks. With the vodka going down much smoother than I expected, four of us piled into their Lada truck and

drove around town visiting friends and eating, not returning until well past midnight. Back at the restaurant, the serving box had been removed from the outdoor eating tables and thin mattresses put in its place. Everybody found a table for himself and fell asleep under the trees.

The restaurant and subsequently the hotel of my first night in Uzbekistan.

My ringing head was awoken at 5 a.m. by the two daughters sweeping the hard dirt floor of the compound and taking water from the flowing stream in the ditch to sprinkle over the dirt to keep the dust down. After settling my dinner and drink bill from the night before and leaving extra money for the bed, I enjoyed a strong cup of coffee and was off.

Bukhara was now an easy one-hour drive in the sunshine. I was happy with myself that I had turned around the night before and stopped for tea. I knew that these situations were far more available than I made the time for. I could not recall any instance when a quick cup of tea with a local had not been a pleasant and positive experience. And yet I had this urge to be tucked away "safely" under a hotel roof with the motorcycle under lock and key. Some nights this prehistoric craving for shelter kept

I did not mind waiting a few days, but my visas – as always–were expiring. I pushed Guillaume to leave quickly and with an afternoon goodbye to Erwan, we sped off for the Pamir Highway and all her glory.

Leaving Dushanbe made us realize that the first challenge of the Pamir was going to be getting to the bloody thing. There is some debate on where the road's western beginning actually is, and most put it in Afghanistan, but for me it was the city of Khorog, a bumpy 20 hours southeast of Dushanbe.

Our first campsite overlooked the Panj River, which acted as the international border between Tajikistan and Afghanistan. Its swirling water would be on our right for the ensuing days as we worked our way south. The mountains on both sides of the river were rocky and bare, but where a spring appeared, lush green areas exploded with cherry and peach trees, private gardens, and wheat and poppy crops. In this region, like many others, water equalled life.

From the city of Khorog, the (mostly) asphalt Pamir Highway leads 310 kilometres east to the town of Murgab. However, long ago I had heard about another, spectacular, U-shaped loop that heads south from Khorog and continues to skirt Afghanistan before looping back east through the Wakhan Valley, reuniting itself with the Pamir Highway halfway to Murgab. We couldn't resist.

Guillaume and I got the maps out and divided this side trip into sections. From Khorog, we followed the river south to the border town of Ishkashim. From there, we would continue east along the Wakhan Valley to the town of Langar before leaving the river and heading north over the Khargush Pass back to the proper Pamir Highway.

We were lucky enough to find ourselves in the small town of Ishkashim for the cross-border market on a Saturday morning, which was held on a large patch of dry riverbed in the no-man's-land between Tajikistan and Afghanistan. We made our way to the market, handing our passports to the guard at the gate to guarantee our return.

Traders from both countries came to make every possible business. All goods were literally carried in from both countries, though only the luckier salespeople had access to a wheelbarrow. There were TVs, spices, hundreds of carpets, pirated DVDs, plastic shoes, and one vendor who brought a huge cooler with ice cream in it. The morning passed quickly as I ate ice cream and voyeuristically watched the negotiation process between the salesmen and the buyers.

The Tajik-Afghan International Saturday market.

By late afternoon Guillaume and I settled into a comfortable third-gear speed and followed the road, and the muddy swirls of the Panj River, east. This river would eventually become the Amu Darya River and – like the Colorado River in the USA – not a drop of it would reach its historical destination (in this case, the shrinking Aral Sea). Heavy irrigation for

OPPOSITE: The muddy water of the Panj River separates Tajikistan (left) and Afghanistan as we head south to the town of Ishkashim.

cotton crops in Tajikistan, Uzbekistan, and Turkmenistan sucked it dry well before then.

We could easily see across the river into Afghanistan as we travelled. The Tajik side had a proper road, electricity and brick houses, while the Afghan side sported mud huts and a single track that hugged the sides of the mountains.

Out of all the roads that I had travelled, I decided that this weeklong route had the potential to benchmark my adventure travelling. The culture and languages were new to me and historically fascinating. The substantial physical distance between the Wakhan Corridor and the outside world creates an enveloping feeling of commitment, and I realized that I could not simply leave, even if I wished to. Erwan's frustrating attempts to return to Europe with his motorcycle convinced me of that – and he was in the capital city. Towns and fuel stops were far apart, so nonchalant travel only welcomed trouble. Emergency international medical assistance was days away; the area's general inaccessibility demanded a serious acceptance of personal responsibility. The amount of paperwork and bureaucracy needed to access the Wahkan Corridor was staggering, but riding there I felt it to be an appropriate price to pay. In fact, it was a bargain.

The high-altitude plateaus and the towering Hindu Kush mountains – separated by Central Asia's mightiest river – left little to improve on in a geographic respect. This land supported a few subsistence farmers and Kyrgyz herders who were proud of their lifestyles, and generations spent living off the meagre offerings of the Pamir mountain range had driven the tradition of hospitality and sharing deep into their culture. A cup of tea was never far away at any stop.

Many travellers, on motorcycles or with backpacks, crave authentic experiences in foreign lands. Our collective brow furrows when the local elder asks us to please exit the village through the gift shop. We choose new destinations hoping that the location will make us feel as if we were the first foreigners ever to show up, and that our excitement to share details of our world will be trumped only by our hosts' excitement to share

Faces from the Wahkan Corridor.

details of theirs.

I know that I have precious few opportunities for these exchanges. Above all else, I want my new friends to know that I, for one, do not want to change the way they think, or to offer quick solutions for their problems. I did want to start to reverse the ages-old experience where two people of different histories meet, only for one to ask or force change from the other. For me, it will be: Greet, share, listen, shake hands, and ride on.

The occasional village along the way had built rock walls beside the road to reduce the dust and noise of the even less occasional traffic. In one nondescript town, Guillaume and I stopped a man and used our sign language to ask for a place to put our tents and sleep for the night. He understood perfectly and turned us immediately into the next driveway. We parked the bikes in the fruit orchard while the women cleaned an area under the mulberry trees to put our tents. I thought the

Guillaume leaving Langar.

Up to the Khargush Pass.

THE UNIVERSITY OF GRAVEL ROADS

ladies were being a little too meticulous in cleaning the ground until I realized that they were not cleaning it for us, they were collecting all the mulberry fruit that had fallen. They were not going to let two strangers squash their next dinner with tents.

Communicating only with hand gestures and phrasebook Tajik, we drank green tea and toured the small farm. We learned that there were

Upon arrival in Murgab, we found a home stay for spending the night, and they fired up the wood-powered hot-water shower. Being thoroughly cleaned and fed, we sat on multiple layers of carpets on the floor and sank into knitted cushions telling tales of the road, and as usual, were supplied endless pots of piping hot green tea.

three families living in the one stone house, and multi-generational families at that. Water came from a narrow stone canal that started up in the hills behind the house and delivered delicious water steadily all day.

Relaxing behind the house in the morning, my journal writing was pleasantly interrupted by the arrival of fresh pots of tea and flat bread made in the clay oven similar to an Indian tandoor. Guillaume got a balloon from his luggage and squeezed in a game of volleyball with the kids before we hit the road.

At Langar we left the river's side for the first time in weeks and turned north towards the Pamir Highway. We wound our way quickly up to 3400 metres (11,155 ft) and would stay near this altitude until the 4,344-metre (14,252 ft) pass at Khargush the next day.

Because of the proximity of the pass to Afghanistan and its drug trade, the Russian military patrolled the area, which included an intimidating document and passport check at the bottom of the pass.

It was a no-nonsense checkpoint with two sets of gates and armed guards stationed behind sandbagged walls. The commander of the post came over once the passport and permit checks were done, shook our hands, and said hello (in Russian, of course).

He thought I was German.

"No, no. Canada. Hockey," I smiled and said.

"Ah, hockey. Gretzky!" he replied.

I could not think of any Russian players in the current league, so I blurted out "Tretiak!" – the amazing goaltender from the 1970s. The commander cracked a smile and we continued to banter back and forth in the international language of hockey players' last names until he waved us on through.

By the afternoon the Pamir Highway was in sight. I had not expected it to be so wide or for the asphalt to be in one piece. However, once I was on it, it felt like the road bed was laid down over huge fluffy pillows as the bike floated up a lump and then down lazily into the next slight depression in the road.

Guillaume and I leap-frogged each other, taking photos, and with only 150 kilometres to Murgab, we were in no hurry to waste the views.

A frosty morning with a deep blue sky greeted us the next day we headed for the 4,655-metre (15,268 ft) Ak-Baital pass. This pass gives the Pamir Highway the designation of the second highest paved highway in the world, just behind the 4,877-metre (15,996 ft) Karakoram highway just over the Chinese border to the east.

This was the Pamir that I had struggled to get to and I was immensely proud that a long string of intentional decisions (and many unintentional ones also) had gotten me to the top of this pass. Snow sat on the moun-

Ak-Baital Pass.

taintops, dirty with spring's dust, and it melted slowly into thin, trickling streams. It was completely barren and breathtaking.

We didn't linger on the pass. We arrived at the Tajik border post at 5:30 in the evening and went through the formalities of leaving Tajikistan. Light snow started to fall as we approached the border. I didn't mind being in the office next to the wood-fired heater as I did paperwork.

We crested the mountain pass between the two countries and the snow turned to rain as we descended a dozen muddy hairpin turns into a grey, overcast valley where the Kyrgyzstan border office was located.

Our first Kyrgyz friend, 5 minutes from the border.

A thorough and time-consuming entry process for entering Kyrgyzstan, including a drug search (the first since Djibouti), lasted into twilight. Not far from the border offices, I stopped to photograph a yurt – the traditional round, felt, portable house – and ended up getting invited in for tea. One teabag was brought out and hot water was poured from a large, plastic flask into eight small cups. The mother did the honours of steeping the tea, which involved long dips of the teabag into Guillaume's and my cups, and quick bounces into the other six. In addition to the tea, they offered large bowls of kumis, a refreshing drink traditionally made

Fresh kumis for sale.

An old proverb claims that "horses are the wings of the Kyrgyz."

of fermented horse's milk. It tasted like bitter skim milk and bubble-less champagne. Surprisingly, it was not at all unpleasant.

After another cup of tea and round of photographs, we excused ourselves and bid our hosts goodnight. We drove 20 minutes to a small café that had a few beds in the back for rent; all the while I wondered how you actually milk a horse.

The closer we came to the capital of Bishkek, the busier the roads got. Families had set up summer yurts in the rolling green hills of the countryside, and it was not uncommon to see an expensive 4x4 parked out-

Fuel stop in the countryside, with both 93 and 80 octane available.

side of the yurt. This reminded me of South Africa, where the BMWs and Mercedes bumped along dirt tracks to return to the village on weekends and holidays, the current generation trying to connect their rural roots to their city lifestyles.

For me, Bishkek was a quick stop to do laundry on my way on up to Almaty, Kazakhstan, where the visa game would continue for Russia and Mongolia. Guillaume did not have his Kazakh visa yet, and he stayed behind to sort that out. I arrived in Almaty after negotiating the easiest border crossing of the entire trip – I did not even have to get off the bike to leave Kyrgyzstan.

Kazakhstan is rich in oil and natural gas, and the old capital city of Almaty is dotted with glass-enclosed shopping malls, indoor skating rinks, and patio cafés with wireless internet access. Many small kiosks along the road and sidewalks sold ice cream and newspapers as well as beer, and drinking in public was not discouraged. Walking downtown on a warm Friday in June, the best (and worst) of Russian fashion was on display and I noted in my journal that the shortness of the skirts hit an all-time high in Almaty.

My motorcycle errands included buying a new battery and picking up my knobby tires that were waiting for me at the post office. I installed the front tire and strapped the rear to the back of the bike, not wanting to wear its tread down on the asphalt roads of Kazakhstan and Russia if I did not have to. I usually disliked carrying tires, but this one was my Mongolian safety blanket.

I took some solace in the fact that this was the last capital city where I needed to expend energy and cash securing visas for upcoming countries. I picked up my Mongolian visa and went to the Russian embassy for my last and most expensive ($380) visa of the trip. I had made it through the worst part of the visa game, and now instead of fretting about visa issues, I was concerned about missing my plane a plane in Vladivostok. That made an uneasy shift in how I approached my routing through Russia and Mongolia, and how much ground I wanted to cover per day. Gone were the days of stopping at picturesque campsites for a few days of baking bread and reading books. I was on the edge of Siberia, months away from finishing, and yet the western world and its schedules were creeping back into my life.

The road to Russia was asphalt and in fair condition, good enough to let me daydream about upcoming Mongolia. My pre-arrival research normally involved mostly practical matters such as visa information, money and fuel facts, not extensive history or geography profiles. Mongolia in particular had been a part of my dream since the initial days spent staring at the atlas back in Colorado Springs, and I enjoyed the fabrication of what I thought was going to be there. I imagined yaks, butter tea, sparsely inhabited plains dotted with the felt tents of nomads. I anticipated its remoteness and the self-sufficiency it would ask of me. I pictured myself making hilltop stops, looking at a maze of tracks heading to the next town, and squinting to see any dust for clues to indicate which track was the correct one. Some travellers investigate their prospective fruits on Google Earth and comb the internet for pictures and detailed descriptions for each kilometre. I did not want the reality of the county to interfere with my personal conception of the place until the last possible moment.

Tajik yurt.

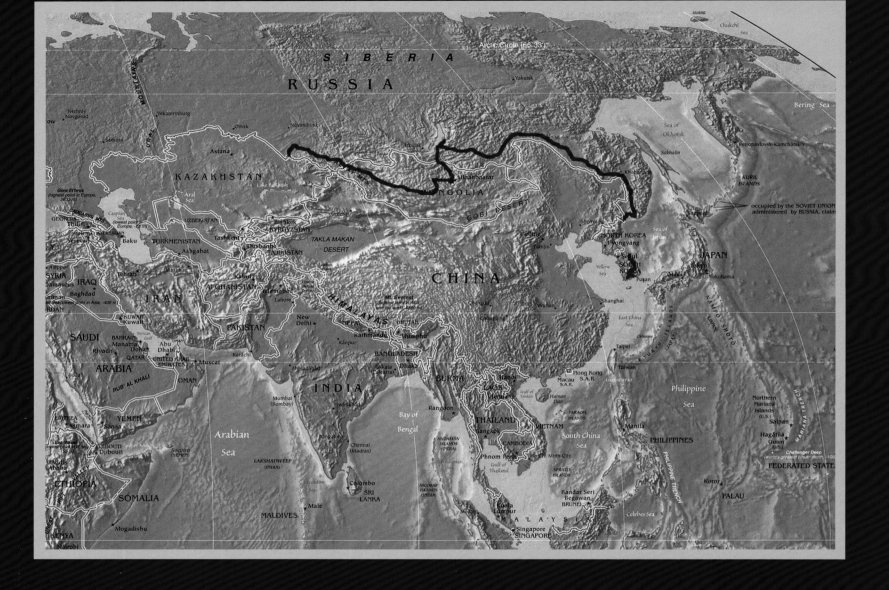

CHAPTER 8
RUSSIA AND MONGOLIA

Kazakhstan and Mongolia are technically separated by only 40 kilometres of Russian territory, but getting to one from the other requires a 900-kilometre hook through southern Russia; there is no direct route. The detour is a scenic one, as it is almost entirely within the Altai Mountains, a rugged range shared by Russia, Mongolia, Kazakhstan, and China.

Streams filtered from the mountains and fed the Chuya River, alongside which ran the main road to Mongolia. Along the riverbanks of the river were many guesthouses and forested camping areas for nearly naked Russian holidaymakers taking advantage of the short but beautiful summer weather. Arriving at one of these campsites as a solo traveller meant vodka, new friends and multiple toasts to many things during the course of an evening. I was in the very southern part of the Siberian Federal District of Russia, but this was not the Siberia I expected. I happily watched as another of my preconceived views dissolved in the light of experience.

I changed my rear tire near the Mongolian border, and gave the motorcycle an appreciative wash. It had 140,000 kilometres on it and was running like a champ. I was happy about that, as two of my most anticipated crossings were yet to come. The 1700-kilometre dirt track from the Mongolian western border to the capital city was one of three must-do roads for me in this part of the world, along with the Pamir Highway and the Trans-Siberian trek from Lake Baikal to Vladivostok, which ominously did not even appear on my road map of Russia.

The Pamir Highway was done, and the Mongolian track was one border crossing away. While filling out immigration paperwork to get into Mongolia, I met Paul and Tim, two middle-aged Englishmen on a charity rally. This is an event where folks buy a 4x4 and drive it at their own pace to Mongolia, where the vehicle is auctioned off and the money goes to local charities. The drivers then fly or otherwise make their way back to the U.K.

We cleared customs together and started into the great plains of Mongolia. My mind reeled at the acknowledgement of where I was. Mongolia was everything that I had hoped it would be. The rolling landscapes, the dirt roads, the yurts (called gers in Mongolia), and animals that dotted the hillsides were all there, just as I imagined. There were, however, two things that struck me as out of place. One was the presence of telephone poles, which of course made sense but had never made it into my romantic vision of the Mongolian countryside.

The second item was the lack of fences. My Canadian eyes were used to seeing wide swathes of countryside, but at home the landscape is segregated, controlled, owned, and divided up. The animal husbandry and herding history of the

Massive wheat farms greeted me as I crossed from Kazakhstan.

Mongol people opposed the chaining up of one's land for personal use only. As a result, the road was not limited to a corridor between fences, but instead went wherever the smoothest driving was. When the tracks became too corrugated or sandy, detour tracks were made around the trouble area and a new road was formed. Wide, short grass plains were full of these multiple tracks, and more often than not they eventually came back on each other.

As a law-abiding westerner, I hesitated to ride outside the established tracks, but when a massive valley presented itself to me on a cool morning, I was able to let go of my road politeness and cut across to the other side, making my own personal road. My new rear tire did wonders for traction in the loose soil and I kept an eye on where the main track was heading and also watched for any rivers or hazards in my way, but the solid ground of perfect off-road riding continued until I looped back to the road. I wondered anachronistically what it would have been like to arrive with a motorcycle in the middle of Canada in the twelfth century, at the same time Genghis Khan was busy here in Mongolia.

ABOVE: Small dark wood houses, backyard water wells and tough-as-nails old ladies puttering in the fence-side garden – this is the Siberia I had imagined.

BELOW: The last road in Russia climbs into the hills where Mongolia awaits.

Canada and Mongolia are at similar latitudes, so would our prairies have yielded a similar ride? Canada's landscape has been manipulated so extensively that was difficult for me to imagine what the area where I

OPPOSITE PAGE: Mongolian road signs were as rare as accurate Mongolian maps.

lived had looked like before intensive farming arrived.

I bumped into Paul and Tim throughout the day and together we arrived into Olgii, the largest town on the western side of the country. On the outskirts of town I ran over a nail and coasted until I saw a tire repair place, while Paul and Tim looked for a shop to replace a rear shock that they had broken earlier in the day. By 8 p.m. our repairs were done and we set up camp a kilometre from town.

As we talked about our travels, it became apparent that they were not entirely prepared for this section of the journey. I was entering coordinates into the GPS unit, and they asked if they should get a map.

"It's 1600 kilometres of dirt road and you guys don't have a map?" I asked in disbelief.

"We do! We have a camping map of Europe, and this Russian atlas with a map of Mongolia in it," they replied simply. "And two compasses."

The Mongolian map in the book was the size of a postcard.

"Uh, yeah, you guys need a map."

They reluctantly agreed and also thought my GPS might come in handy, which was part of the reason we travelled together for the next

Old man enjoying the market.

four days.

I welcomed the chance to have them tag along. Paul was a retired newspaper photographer and I desperately wanted this section of the trip to be documented with as many photos as I could. As an added bonus, they could carry my beer in their truck.

There are many road maps of Mongolia. However, the simple fact of their existence does not mean that they are accurate. Similarly, a road that appears on a Mongolian map cannot be assumed to exist in real life. Perhaps it once did, but the roads have a life of their own – twisting, bending and changing course with time. My GPS couldn't help much, as it only told me the direction of the next town's waypoint, which was often hundreds of kilometres away.

For this reason, leaving a town was always more difficult than entering it. When leaving, we were faced with literally dozens of tracks, each looking as if it could be the right one. As long as they went in the general direction of the next town, I was happy. The local drivers did not use maps. They would drive for five kilometres in the direction that they wanted to go, then stop at a ger to ask for directions, repeating as necessary. My Mongolian was not good enough for that, and we suffered the old-fashioned way.

The road quality was completely unpredictable. Smooth tracks would abruptly give way to rocky sections of washboard. In general, the tracks that wandered through the fields were in much better condition than those where there had been some attempts at road building. Previous construction tended to produce a road that was wide and straight, but nastily grooved with heavy corrugations. Everybody but the big tanker

There are many roads in Mongolia, but very, very, few of them are paved. The collection of gers in the middle would serve as a teahouse, restaurant, bar, and expensive, emergency fuel depot.

OPPOSITE: Dodging storms.

LEFT: At a rare ger stop to ask for directions, we are invited in and I attempt a conversation using the Mongolian phrase book. On the table are salted, milky tea, dried cheese from curdled milk, and bread – all wonderfully flavourful.

TOP: Sunset signals the return to the camp for the night.

BOTTOM: No fences, no traffic lights.

Every chance I could, I dipped into the local streams to get the dust from the tracks off.

trucks weaved rollercoaster-like along the sides of the main road on makeshift detours, carving out as smooth a ride as possible.

The stretches of land and sky that were visible from the bike continually amazed me. It was possible to see storms brewing far off on the horizon and track their progress as they lumbered across the land. After a few stretches of wet, slippery roads we learned that the best way to deal with the rain was to avoid it. This was what busted Ewan and Charlie in *The Long Way Round*. If they had had more time, they could have found a ger, said hello, and gone inside to drink Mongolian tea, a weak, milky affair that often had a dollop of salted butter in it. If they had had a few spare weeks, they could have stuck their heads out after every few cups and continued on their way when the storm had passed.

Tim, Paul and I fell into a routine of having the motorcycle and its GPS in front, the truck following. Having the GPS did not prevent me from taking a wrong track. I could see the road that we wanted five kilometres away on the other side of a shallow valley, but as we got further into the valley, we realized it was a catch basin for large hills on either side. We had driven into the mother of all bogs. I kept waiting for a road to cut across the valley to connect the two sides, but it never appeared.

We admitted defeat when the truck sank to its axles in mud and we lost the daylight. Tim was anxious to keep moving, being quite adamant that we could not stay where we were because there were too many mosquitoes. I couldn't possibly imagine where else he thought we could go and dismissed the complaining as his version of self-therapy. We set up camp in the dark and I assembled my tent wearing all of my gear – including my helmet – to keep the mosquitoes at bay. There was no lingering outside and enjoying the stars. Tim kept us awake as he slapped away at

ABOVE: The sidestand has taken a beating on this trip, and this is the fourth time it has come off to get repaired. One of the tabs holding on the sidestand spring had broken off. In the rain the welders tacked on a new tab and closed another crack on the stand for $1.

BELOW: I eat buuz while Tim and Paul go looking for spare tires. Buuz are dumplings made from a filling of mutton and fat and then steamed. On the table are soy sauce and a generic hot sauce to slather them with. At $0.20 each, they are cheap and a warming treat on a cold, wet day.

the ceiling of the truck, trying to kill the bugs that were shut in the truck with him so he could get some sleep. The next morning a three-hour backtrack was needed to get back onto the correct road, but once on it, we made good time east.

Paul, Tim and I followed a pattern of driving steadily but at a reasonable pace. Cargo trucks made the 1600-kilometre run from Olgii to the capital city of Ulaanbaatar in six days, and we were estimating eight. We planned to finish most nights by 6 p.m., but often went later because of not wanting to stop in a stormy area, or because somebody was eager to have a beer at the next town.

Accommodation was easy to find, because Mongolia is the best country in the world for camping. There are plenty of streams coming down out of the mountains for washing and cooking, and these little flood zones often have grass growing on the edges, so they are perfect places to set up tents. Curious locals regularly came over to look at the motorcycle and say hello, but there were never any issues with safety.

After five days of travelling together, we pitched up at a riverside camping spot in Bayankhongor, where two more teams from the charity rally found us and we had an idyllic evening on the side of the river. Meeting the other rally contestants gave Paul, Tim, and me the chance to go our separate ways. The boys could travel in a convoy with the other trucks, and if they got separated from each other it was only 200 kilometres to the next town, where a paved road could take them into Ulaanbaatar.

Every day brought me closer to the city of Ulaanbaatar, but I was not ready to finish this run of spectacular roads and scenery, so I added side trips to temples and monasteries where I could. During one of my wandering detours, the smell of rain arrived on a new wind from the west.

LEFT, TOP: Local horsemen were always drawn to the motorcycle, especially interested in the large knobby tires. 125cc Chinese and Russian motorcycles were common to see near the smaller towns and popped up in the most remote places, usually with two or three people aboard.

LEFT, MIDDLE: In the morning, this young man stopped by to say hello on his way to work with the goats.

LEFT, BOTTOM: Happy to look at the bike, happy to talk in sign language, and happy to smile for the camera; what a life.

UPPER LEFT: A young girl waits for her father in his Uaz, a sturdy Russian-built 4x4.

UPPER RIGHT: A village in the middle of a long stretch of road provides a rest stop for drivers. The trucks in the background are carrying heaping mounds of raw cashmere, likely destined for processing in China.

LOWER LEFT: Moving day for a truck, trailer and tractor.

LOWER MIDDLE: Afternoon rain keeps the dust down.

LOWER RIGHT: On a local truck, a spray-painted CCCP (Union of Soviet Socialist Republics) sign testifies to the close relationship between the Soviet Union and Mongolia until the Mongolian Democratic Revolution in 1990.

Clouds grew and their appearance removed the comforting sunshine that had been with me since the morning. Across the valley, I saw two riders on horseback, their hats pulled down low over their faces and their waistcoats shut tight to keep the headwind and spitting rain out. I raised a hand in greeting, and they returned the gesture, careful not to raise their

Shankh Khiid Monastery. In the 16th century, Buddhism became the state religion, although religious freedom was widely accepted for 400 more years. This changed dramatically in 1937, when Stalin wiped out 700 monasteries in Mongolia and killed an estimated 20,000 monks. The democracy movement in 1990 led to the opening of several hundred monasteries, including Shankh Khiid, one of the few surviving original monasteries.

arms too much for fear of breaking the seals on their jackets to the wind. As the rain began to pelt me, I imagined this spirit of camaraderie going on for hundreds of years before our little interchange: riders travelling in opposite directions to unknown destinations, strangers lifting a hand as if to say "My friend, I wish you well on your journey, go safely home to your family." At least that was what I was wishing to the anonymous rider across the valley, and I hoped he was wishing the same for me.

On the overcast days, I spent hours in isolated roadside cafés, drinking tea, waiting for the rain clouds to move out of my intended path. This was more of an excuse to remain in the tea houses writing in my journal and watching the locals than any attempt to avoid getting wet. On sunny days, in late afternoon, the sun lost the intense heat it had inflicted during the day, and made amends by bathing the hills and plains in golden light. There were many times, driving slowly through picturesque fields of grasses and wildflowers with nobody around me, that I told myself to stop and write down exactly what I was seeing and thinking about this spectacular run. How I was going to try and re-tell it? There were so many analogies that I wanted to record, and I was afraid that the more of them filled my helmet, the more I was going to forget.

Arriving in Ulaanbaatar was bittersweet; although I was happy to be there, I was a touch sad at having to get there so quickly. I found a small guesthouse and after a shower, laundry, and a beer, I got down to the internet. The paperwork involved with getting to Alaska had been piling up while I was in the countryside. It appeared that shipping by plane from eastern Russia to Alaska was out. The cargo company responsible for getting the motorcycle to Alaska had raised the price on the shipment quote, and my meagre remaining budget forced me to cut out the Alaska leg that I had planned. I cancelled my passenger ticket from Vladivostok to Alaska and made plans to take a ferry from Vladivostok to South Korea instead. From there, I could place the motorcycle in a crate, send it to any American west coast sea terminal, and drive home. There was always the option of sending the motorcycle directly to Vancouver by sea, but that seemed a distasteful way to end the trip. I did not want to fly to Vancouver, enter my home country at the airport and take the bus down to the port to collect the bike. I had been through 52 border crossings by land, and I wanted to hear the stamp-stamp-stamp of my final crossing into Canada with the motorcycle by my side.

On the morning before leaving, I noticed fresh drops of coolant under

accuracy, and public cleanliness. After just a brief tour, I psyched myself up for yet another paperwork nightmare involving crating and ocean shipping. It turned out to be embarrassingly easy to organize the shipment to California, and in September, I returned to the USA.

The legendary leader of the Mongol people, Genghis Khan.

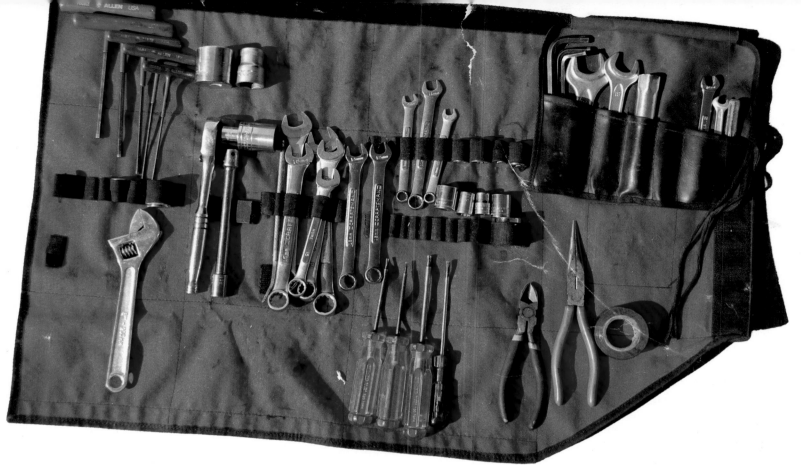

OPPOSITE: Maintenance schedule, 2003-2008.

ABOVE: In my tankbag I carried the small black roll, which held most things I needed to take the wheels off and small maintenance jobs: 8mm/10mm wrench, 13mm wrench, small cable ties, sparkplug tool, 4-5-6-8 Allen, Torx folding tool set (not pictured), screwdriver with combination Phillips and flathead tips (not pictured), 19mm wrench, 24mm wrench.

At the bottom of one of the panniers was the big tool roll. The roll itself is from Touratech. It contained wrenches 8-9-10-11-12-13-14-15-16-17-22, 3/8" drive ratchet, 6" extension, and sockets 8-9-10-11-12-13-14-15-16-17-19-21-22, and 15/16" for the sump plug, T-handle allen wrenches 2.5-3-4-5-6, Torx screwdrivers 15-20-25-30, crescent wrench, needle nose pliers, side cutters, and a small round file.

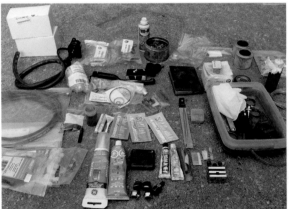

LEFT: Spare Parts Inventory, This list grew or shrank depending on how far from civilization I was going: rear sub-frame bolts, WD-40, mirror bolt, small tin of miscellaneous bolts, washers and clamps, air filters, short length of fuel hose, radiator fan motor without the fan, front and rear brake pads, clutch lever, water pump shaft and seals, sump plug, digital multimeter, replacement bulbs, oil filters, electrical tape, 15 tooth countershaft sprocket, lock washer for the countershaft sprocket, small tube of automatic transmission fluid to lubricate the chain, tie wire, latex gloves, spare Sidi buckles, feeler gauges, spare master links, valve cores, fuse kit, dental pick, razor blades, chain break, anti-seize crayon, J-B Weld, blue and red thread locker, folding magnifying glass, gasket maker, silicone, dielectric grease, film canisters of Motol 300 high temp grease, cable ties, TDC pin, valve shims, O-ring kits, clutch and throttle cables, fuel filter. Not pictured are front and rear tubes.

As part of the flat repair kit I carried multiple tubes of glue and multiple patches. I had CO2 cartridges and a small bicycle pump for inflation. The three tire irons I kept in the ABS tool roll under the radiator along with two tie-down straps.

FOLLOWING PAGE: A rest stop in Inner Mongolia.